Andrew:	Now, now. I thought you were well brought up. Surely you know it's very rude to make personal remarks.
Milo:	I'm sorry. You were disparaging my lover.
Andrew:	On the contrary, I was reminiscing about my wife . . .

SLEUTH
Anthony Shaffer's smash Broadway play

A thriller about the game—Sex—the penalty—Marriage—and the remedy—Murder . . .

"One of the slickest and best written mystery plays to come along!"

—New York

"Literate, witty, scary and filled with sudden twists and tricks . . . One of the best!"

—New York Daily News

"Ranks with those English thriller classics **Witness for the Prosecution** and **Dial M for Murder** . . . **SLEUTH** will keep you limp, scared, happy, on your toes, surprised and fooled and most of all, entertained!"

—Peggy Stockton, WMCA

"A slick breathless extravaganza . . . Reads better than most popular novels!"

—Chicago Skyline

PALOMAR PICTURES INTERNATIONAL
presents

LAURENCE OLIVIER   MICHAEL CAINE

in

JOSEPH L. MANKIEWICZ' film of

Sleuth

Based on the play by
ANTHONY SHAFFER

Screenplay by
ANTHONY SHAFFER

Executive Producer
EDGAR J. SCHERICK

Produced by
MORTON GOTTLIEB

Directed by
JOSEPH L. MANKIEWICZ

Released by
TWENTIETH CENTURY-FOX

Color by Deluxe ®

Sleuth

ANTHONY SHAFFER

BANTAM BOOKS
TORONTO · NEW YORK · LONDON
A NATIONAL GENERAL COMPANY

SLEUTH

*A Bantam Book / published by arrangement with
Dodd, Mead & Company*

PRINTING HISTORY
*Dodd, Mead edition published December 1970
2nd printing . . . September 1971
3rd printing . . . June 1972
Bantam edition published December 1972*

TO

Father Brown, Mr. Philip Trent, Mr. Max Carrados, Dr. Reginald Fortune, Mr. Roger Sheringham, Mr. Albert Campion, Mr. Nigel Strangeways, Lord Peter Wimsey, Dr. Gideon Fell, Monsieur Hercule Poirot, and all their omniscient, eccentric, amateur gentlemen colleagues, this play is dedicated with sincere regard and affection.

SLEUTH was first produced by Michael White at the St. Martin's Theatre, London, on February 12, 1970. The cast was as follows:

ANDREW WYKE	*Anthony Quayle*
MILO TINDLE	*Keith Baxter*
INSPECTOR DOPPLER	*Stanley Rushton*
DETECTIVE SERGEANT TARRANT	*Robin Mayfield*
POLICE CONSTABLE HIGGS	*Liam McNulty*

Directed by Clifford Williams
Designed by Carl Toms
Lighting by Francis Reid

SLEUTH was produced on Broadway by Helen Bon-
fils, Morton Gottlieb, and Michael White at the Music
Box Theater on November 12, 1970, with the following
cast:

ANDREW WYKE	*Anthony Quayle*
MILO TINDLE	*Keith Baxter*
INSPECTOR DOPPLER	*Philip Farrar*
DETECTIVE SERGEANT	
TARRANT	*Harold K. Newman*
POLICE CONSTABLE HIGGS	*Roger Purnell*

Directed by Clifford Williams
Designed by Carl Toms (American
supervision by William Ritman)
Lighting by William Ritman

SCENE: *Andrew Wyke's country home in Wiltshire, England*

ACT ONE: *A summer evening*

ACT TWO: *Two days later*

ACT ONE

The living room of Andrew Wyke's Norman Manor House in Wiltshire, England. It is stone flagged, and a tall window runs the height of the back wall. It is divided laterally by a minstrels gallery which, in turn, is approached by a winding staircase. A wardrobe, stage left, and a grandfather clock, and bureau stage right stand on the gallery. Upstage right is the hallway leading to the unseen front door. Upstage left a corridor leads into another part of the house. Standing in this corridor is a large basket hamper. Games of all kinds adorn the room, ranging in complexity from chess, draughts and checkers, to early dice and card games and even earlier blocking games like Senat and Nine Men Morris. Sitting by the window, under the gallery, is a life-sized figure of a Laughing Sailor.

A summer evening.

ANDREW WYKE *is sitting at his desk, typing. He is a strongly built, tall, fleshy man of fifty-seven, gone slightly to seed. His fair hair carries on it the suspicion that chemical aid has been invoked to keep the*

1

grey at bay. His face, sourly amused and shadowed with evaded self-knowledge, is beginning to reflect the absence of constant, arduous employment. He wears a smoking jacket and black tie.

The clock strikes eight o'clock. ANDREW *turns to look at clock, finishes typing, takes the page from the typewriter and begins to read.*

ANDREW: "Since you appear to know so much, Lord Merridew, sir," said the Inspector humbly, "I wonder if you could explain just how the murderer managed to leave the body of his victim in the middle of the tennis court, and effect his escape without leaving any tracks behind him in the red dust. Frankly, sir, we in the Police Force are just plain baffled. There seems no way he could have done it, short of black magic." St. John Lord Merridew, the great detective, rose majestically, his huge Father Christmas face glowing with mischievous delight. Slowly he brushed the crumbs of seedy cake from the folds of his pendulous waistcoat. "The police may be baffled, Inspector," he boomed, "but Merridew is not. It's all a question of a little research and a little ratiocination. Thirty years ago, the murderer, Doctor Grayson, was a distinguished member of the Ballets Russes, dancing under the name of Oleg

Graysinski. The years may have altered his appearance, but his old skill had not deserted him. He carried the body out to the center of the tennis court, walking on his points along the white tape which divides the service boxes. From there he threw it five feet into the court, towards the base line, where it was found, and then, with a neatly executed fouetté, faced about and returned the way he had come, thus leaving no traces. There, Inspector, that is Merridew's solution."

[*He picks up his drink*]

Splendid! Absolutely splendid! Merridew loses none of his cunning, I'm glad to say. He's as neat *and* as gaudy as ever he was.

[*The doorbell rings.* ANDREW *finishes his drink slowly, then exits to hallway*]

ANDREW: [*Offstage in hall*] Oh hullo. Good evening, Milo Tindle, is it?

MILO: [*Offstage in hall*] Yes. Mr. Wyke?

ANDREW: Yes. Do come in, won't you?

MILO: Thank you.

3

[*The front door is heard to close.* ANDREW *walks back into the room, followed by* MILO TINDLE. *He is about thirty-five, slim, dark-haired and of medium height. He has a sharp, sallow face alive with a faintly Mediterranean wariness. Everything about him is neat, from his exactly parted hair to the squared-off white handerchief in the breast pocket of his blue mohair suit*]

ANDREW: Let me take your coat. [*He hangs coat on coat rack*] Did you find the entrance to the lane all right?

MILO: Yes. [*He walks about surveying room*]

ANDREW: Well done. Most people go straight past it. It's very nice of you to come.

MILO: Not at all. I found your note when I got down from London this afternoon.

ANDREW: Oh good. I pushed it through your letter box.

MILO: Er . . . What's this? [*He indicates the figure of the Laughing Sailor*]

ANDREW: Oh that's Jolly Jack Tar the Jovial Sailor. He and I have a very good relationship. I make the jokes and he laughs at them. [*He moves the sailor's head manually*] You see, ha-ha-ha! Now let me get you a drink. [*He crosses to drinks table*] What will you have? Scotch, gin, vodka?

MILO: Scotch.

ANDREW: How do you like it? Soda, water, ice?

MILO: Just ice. And what's this?

[MILO *has crossed to a table on which there is a large game*]

ANDREW: Oh, that's a game.

MILO: A child's game. [*He picks up one of the pieces*]

ANDREW: It's anything but childish, I can assure you. I've been studying it for months, and I'm still only a novice. It's called Senat, played by the ancient Egyptians. It's an early blocking game, not unlike our own Nine Men Morris. Would you mind putting that back where you found it? It's taken me a long time to get it there. How are you settling in at Laundry Cottage?

MILO: Very well.

ANDREW: Using it for weekends, that sort of thing?

MILO: Yes, that's the sort of thing.

ANDREW: It's a charming little place. Well, cheers.

MILO: Cheers.

ANDREW: Now do come and sit down. Forgive me if I just tidy up a bit. I've just reached the denouement of my new book. "The Body On the Tennis Court." Tell me, would you agree that the detective story is the normal recreation of noble minds?

MILO: Who said that?

ANDREW: Oh, I'm quoting Philip Guedalla. A biographer of the thirties. The golden age when every cabinet minister had a thriller by his bedside, and all the detectives were titled. Before your time, I expect.

MILO: Perhaps it would have been truer to say that noble minds were the normal recreation of detective story writers.

ANDREW: Yes. Good point. You know, even in these days I still set my own work among the gentry. And a great number of people enjoy it, in spite of the Welfare State.

MILO: I'm surprised they haven't done any of your stuff on television.

ANDREW: Oh, God forbid.

MILO: Well, they're always doing crime stories.

ANDREW: What—you mean those ghastly things where the police race around in cars and call all the suspects chummy?

MILO: Yes. That's the kind of thing.

ANDREW: Oh no. That's not my line of country at all. That is detective fact, not detective fiction.

MILO: And of course as such is of much less interest to noble minds.

ANDREW: Yes, yes, you've put it in a nutshell, my dear Milo, if I may so address you?

MILO: Of course.

ANDREW: Thank you, we need to be friendly. Now do sit down and let me get you another drink. I'm one up on you already. [MILO *starts to sit in chair below staircase.* ANDREW *moves to drinks table*] I understand you want to marry my wife. [*A pause.* MILO *is disconcerted by the directness of the question*] You'll forgive me raising the matter, but as Marguerite is away for a few days, she's up in the North you know, visiting some relatives.

MILO: Is she?

ANDREW: Yes, so I thought it an appropriate time for a little chat.

MILO: Yes.

ANDREW: Well, is it true?

MILO: Well . . . Well, yes, with your permission of course.

ANDREW: Oh, yes, of course. [*He crosses to* MILO *with his drink*] Zere, put zat behind your necktie.

MILO: Cheers.

ANDREW: Prost. [*He stands in front of fireplace*] Yes, I'm glad to see you're not like so many young men these days, seem to think they can do anything they like without asking anyone's permission.

MILO: Certainly not.

ANDREW: Good. I'm pleased to hear it. I know you won't object then if I ask you a few questions about your parents and so on.

MILO: My mother was born in Hereford, a farmer's daughter. My father is an Italian who came to this country in the thirties.

ANDREW: Jewish?

MILO: Half, on his mother's side, that for the Fascists

was the important side. The male, they felt, didn't transmit the disease so virulently.

ANDREW: [*Tut-tutting*] Dreadful business, dreadful.

MILO: Of course I'm not at all religious myself. I'm an agnostic.

ANDREW: [*Crosses to center of room*] My dear boy, you don't have to explain to me. We're all liberals here. I have no prejudice against Jews, or even half-Jews. Why some of my best friends are half-Jews . . . Mind you, I hope you have no objections to any children that you and my wife may have being brought up Church of England?

MILO: None whatsoever if that's what Marguerite wants.

ANDREW: You haven't discussed it yet?

MILO: Not yet, it doesn't seem to have cropped up.

ANDREW: Well, I suppose in some ways that's rather a relief. But if you take my advice, you'll opt for the Established Church. It's so much simpler. A couple of hours on Christmas Eve and Good Friday and you've seen the whole thing off nicely. And if you throw in Remembrance Sunday, they give you the Good Christian medal with oak leaf cluster.

MILO: It's the same with a lot of Jews. My father used to say, "Most people only talk to their really old friends two or three times a year. Why should God be angry if He gets the same treatment?"

ANDREW: [*Insincerely*] Very amusing. Your father? Was his name Tindle? It doesn't sound very Italian.

MILO: His name was Tindolini. But if you had a name like that in England in those days, you had to make a-da-nice cream. He was a watchmaker and so he changed it.

ANDREW: Was he a successful man?

MILO: No. His business failed. He went back to Italy. I send him money from time to time and go and visit him and get a little sun or skiing, depending, of course, on the season.

ANDREW: Ah!

MILO: It's not that I'm disloyal to Britain, you understand. It's just that the Scottish Highlands and Brighton don't offer the same attractions.

ANDREW: And you? What do you do?

MILO: I'm in the travel business. I have my own agency in Dulwich.

ANDREW: Tindle's Travels, eh? I see, and where do you live?

MILO: I live above the office.

ANDREW: In Dulwich?

MILO: Yes, I rent the whole house. It's really most convenient, and . . . and it's most attractive, too. It's Georgian.

ANDREW: H'm, I'm sure it's perfectly delightful, but I doubt whether an eighteenth-century architectural gem in Dulwich whispers quite the same magic to Marguerite as it does to you.

MILO: She adores old houses. She can't wait to live there.

ANDREW: I understood she was already living there— at least for a couple of nights a week. I'm not mistaken, am I? [MILO *shrugs in embarrassment*] And surely your motive in renting the cottage down here was to increase the incidence of this hebdomadal coupling?

MILO: I came to be near the woman I love. It is a great pain for us to be apart. You wouldn't understand.

ANDREW: Possibly. But I understand Marguerite well enough to know that she does not adore old houses.

She's lived here quite a time, and between them the rising damp and the deathwatch beetle have put the boot into her good and proper. She's only got to see a mullioned window and it brings her out in lumps.

MILO: [*Hotly*] Perhaps it wasn't the house so much as the person she had to share it with.

ANDREW: Now, now. I thought you were well brought up. Surely you know it's very rude to make personal remarks.

MILO: I'm sorry. You were disparaging my lover.

ANDREW: On the contrary, I was reminiscing about my wife.

MILO: It comes to the same thing.

ANDREW: Things mostly do, you know. I'll wager that within a year, it's *you* who will be doing the disparaging, and *I* who will be doing the rhapsodizing, having quite forgotten how intolerably tiresome, vain, spendthrift, self-indulgent and generally bloody crafty she really is.

MILO: If you don't love Marguerite, you don't have to abuse her.

ANDREW: Never speak ill of the deadly, eh?

MILO: Now look here . . .

ANDREW: If I choose to say that my wife converses like a child of six, cooks like a Brightlingsea landlady, and makes love like a coelacanth, I shall.

MILO: That's just about enough . . .

ANDREW: And I certainly don't need her lover's permission to do so either. In fact, the only thing I need to know from you is, can you afford to take her off my hands?

MILO: Afford to . . .

ANDREW: Afford to support her in the style to which she wasn't accustomed before she met me, but now is.

MILO: [*Gestures around the room*] She won't need all this when we're married. It'll be a different life—a life of love and simplicity. Now go ahead—sneer at that. It's almost a national sport in this country—sneering at love.

ANDREW: I don't have to sneer at it. I simply don't believe you. For Marguerite, love is the fawning of a willing lap dog, and simplicity a square cut ten-carat diamond from Van Cleef and Arpels.

[MILO *rises to his feet, and moves to drinks table to put down glass*]

MILO: I don't know what I'm doing here. With a little effort I'm sure you could find a much more appreciative audience.

ANDREW: Oh now, Milo. You disappoint me. Rising to your feet like that and *bridling*.

MILO: [*Abashed*] I wasn't bridling. I was protesting.

ANDREW: It looked like a good old-fashioned Hedy Lamarr bridle to me.

MILO: [*Turning to* ANDREW] Who?

ANDREW: Oh, very good! Very good! Why don't you just sit down and we'll talk about something that matters desperately to both of us.

MILO: Marguerite?

ANDREW: Money! Have you got any?

MILO: Well I'm not a millionaire, but I've got the lease on the house and some capital equipment, and the turnover in the business this year has been growing every month. By this time next year I . . .

ANDREW: This year, next year, sometime never. What you're saying in fact is that at present you're skint.

MILO: I'll survive.

ANDREW: I'm sure you will, but survival is not the point. Presumably when you're married to Marguerite you'll want a fast car, a little place in the sun, and a couple of mistresses.

MILO: Why "presumably"? Just because you need those things.

ANDREW: Certainly I do. And so does every right-thinking, insecure, deceitful man. The point is how to get them. [*He moves to drinks table*]

MILO: I'm sure you do all right. [*He crosses to fireplace*]

ANDREW: Me? Oh NO. Just this fading mansion, the slowest Bentley in Wiltshire, and only one mistress, I'm afraid.

MILO: Tea? The Finnish lady who runs the sauna bath at Swindon.

ANDREW: Oh, so you know about her, do you?

MILO: Marguerite and I have no secrets from each other.

ANDREW: Not even mine, it seems. [*Mock mystical*] Te̅a is a Karelian Goddess. Her mother was Ilma, supreme divinity of the air; her father was Jumala, the great Creator. Her golden hair smells of pine, and her cobalt eyes are the secret forest pools of Finlandia.

MILO: I hear she's a scrubbed blonde with all the sex appeal of chilled Lysol.

ANDREW: [*With dignity*] There are those who believe that cleanliness is next to sexiness. And if I were you, I wouldn't pay much attention to what Marguerite says. You can take it from me that Te̅a's an engaging little trollop, and she suits me mightily. Mind you, she takes a bit of keeping up with; it's a good thing I'm pretty much of an Olympic sexual athlete.

MILO: I suppose these days you're concentrating on the sprints rather than the long distance stuff.

ANDREW: Not so, dear boy. [*He sits*] I'm in the pink of condition. I could copulate for England at any distance.

MILO: Well, they do say in Olympic circles, that the point is to take part, rather than to win, so I suppose there's hope for us all. Are you going to marry her?

ANDREW: Marry a goddess? I wouldn't presume. I might get turned into a birch tree for my audacity. Oh, no, I simply want to live with her.

MILO: So what's stopping you?

ANDREW: Basically the firm of Prurient and Pry Ltd., whom you and Marguerite have seen fit to employ. Don't look so innocent. Those nicotine-stained private detectives who've been camping outside Tea's flat for the last week.

MILO: [Crossing to center of room] So you spotted them?

ANDREW: A Bantu with glaucoma couldn't have missed them. No one can read the Evening News for four hours in a Messerschmitt bubble car, and expect to remain undetected.

MILO: Sorry about that. It was Marguerite's idea.

ANDREW: Who else's? Who paid?

MILO: I did.

ANDREW: I wonder you could afford it.

MILO: It was an insurance policy against you changing your mind about divorcing Marguerite.

ANDREW: My dear boy, let us have no misunderstanding. I've nothing against you marrying Marguerite. There's nothing I want more than to see you two tucked up together. But it's got to be a fixture. I want to be rid of her for life, not just a two-week Tindle Tour, economy class. No, you listen to me. You don't know her like I do. You think you do, but you don't. The real truth of the matter is that if you fail her, by which I mean canceling the account at Harrods, or shortchanging her on winter in Jamaica, she'll be back to me in a jiffy, mewing for support—and guilty wife or no, she may be entitled to get it.

MILO: Don't be so bloody pathetic. Winter in Jamaica? I'm not going to take her for winter in Jamaica. You're worrying unnecessarily. Once Marguerite is married to me she'll never think of returning to you. Never. And don't worry about my being able to look after her either.

ANDREW: I see. You mean that as soon as you and she are married, Marguerite will joyously substitute plain water in the bath for her customary asses milk?

MILO: So she's used to luxury. Whose fault is that?

ANDREW: It's not a fault if you can afford it. But can you? Knowing you to be hard up has she shown any sign of mending her ways in these last idyllic three months? Come on now, let's get down to the good guts of the matter. When did she last turn down Bolinger for the blandishments of Babycham? Or reject crêpes suzette in favor of roly-poly? No, no, I'm not joking, how much has this brief liaison cost you so far? Five hundred pounds? eight hundred, a thousand? And that father of yours in Italy, when did you last send him any money? You see why I'm concerned. I tell you. She'll ruin you. To coin a phrase, in two years you'll be a used gourd. And what's more, a used gourd with a sizable overdraft.

MILO: We've often talked about money. I've told her we spend too much.

ANDREW: And she takes no notice?

MILO: [Low] None.

ANDREW: A silvery laugh? A coquettish turn of the head?

MILO: Something like that.

ANDREW: Exactly. Well, it's to solve this little problem that I have invited you here tonight. This, as they say, is where the plot thickens.

MILO: Ah!

ANDREW: I'll get you another drink. [*He crosses to drinks table. In "Listen with Mother" style:*] Are you sitting comfortably? Then I'll begin. Once upon a time there was an Englishman called Andrew Wyke who, in common with most of his countrymen, was virtually castrated by taxation. To avoid total emasculation, his accountants advised him, just before the last devaluation, to put a considerable part of his money, some 135,000 pounds, into jewelry. His wife, of course, was delighted.

MILO: You made her a present of it?

ANDREW: Absolutely not. It's still mine, as well she knows. But we felt she might as well wear it, as bank it. After all, it's fully insured.

MILO: I see what you mean by the plot thickening. It usually does when insurance is mentioned.

ANDREW: I'm glad you follow me so readily. I want you to steal that jewelry.

MILO: [*Astounded*] What?

ANDREW: Tonight, for choice. Marguerite is out of the house. It's an admirable opportunity.

MILO: You must be joking.

ANDREW: You would know it if I were.

MILO: [*Playing for time*] But . . . But what about the servants?

ANDREW: I've sent Mr. and Mrs. Hawkins to the seaside for a forty-eight-hour paddle. They won't be back till Sunday night. So, the house is empty.

MILO: I see.

ANDREW: What do you say?

MILO: It sounds criminal.

ANDREW: Of course it's criminal. All good money-making schemes in England have *got* to be these days. The jewelry, when it's not in the bank, lives in the safe under the stairs. It's there now. All you have to do is steal them, and sell them abroad and live happily ever after with Marguerite. All I have to do is to claim the insurance money and live happily ever after with Teã. [*Pause*] Well, in my case perhaps, not ever after, but at least until I get fed up with a cuisine based on the elk.

MILO: Is that what you asked me over to hear? A scummy little plot to defraud the insurance company?

ANDREW: I'm sorry you find the plot scummy. I thought it was nicely clear and simple.

MILO: Nicely obvious and clearly unworkable. Supposing I do as you say and take the jewels. If I sell them under my own name, I'll be picked up just as soon as you report their loss. If I sell them to a fence, always supposing I could find one, I'd get a fraction of their value.

ANDREW: Not with the fences I know.

MILO: [*Derisory*] What fences would you know?

ANDREW: I know some of the finest fences in Europe. Prudent yet prodigal. I met them some years ago while researching "The Deadly Affair of the Druce Diamond."

MILO: Never read it.

ANDREW: Pity, it was an absolute fizzer—sold a hundred-thousand copies. Anyway on your behalf I have already contacted a certain gentleman in Amsterdam. He will treat you very well; you won't get full value of the jewels but you will get two-thirds, say ninety-thousand pounds, and you'll get it in cash.

MILO: Why should this man be so generous?

ANDREW: Because he will have what fences never

have—title to the jewels. I will see to it that in addition to the jewels, you also steal the receipts I got for them. All you have to do is hand them over together. Now what does my insurance company discover when it swings into action, antennae pulsing with suspicion? It discovers that someone impersonating Andrew Wyke sold the jewels for ninety-thousand pounds cash. They've still got to pay me. Hard cheese. Think it over. Take your time. There's no hurry.

[*A pause.* MILO *considers the proposition.* ANDREW *walks away from* MILO, *humming lightly to himself. He stops by a roll-a-penny wall game and plays it to a successful conclusion.* MILO *paces up and down, indecisive. He suddenly turns and faces* ANDREW]

MILO: Look, I know this sounds stupid, but . . . but well, have you had any experience—I mean, have you ever actually committed a crime before?

ANDREW: Only in the mind's eye, so to speak. For the purpose of my books. St. John Lord Merridew would have a pretty lean time of it if I didn't give him any crime to solve.

MILO: Who?

ANDREW: My detective, St. John Lord Merridew. Known to millions all over the civilized world. "An ambulatory tun of port with the face of Father Christmas." That's how I describe him. "A classical scholar with a taste for good pipes and bad puns, but with a nose for smelling out evil, superior to anything in the force."

MILO: Oh, yes, the police are always stupid in your kind of story, aren't they? They never solve anything. Only an amateur sleuth ever knows what's happening. But that is detective fiction. This is fact.

ANDREW: I am aware of the difference, Milo. I also know that insurance investigators are sharp as razors, and that's why, as Queen Victoria said to Lord Melbourne on the occasion of her coronation, everything's got to be done kosher and according to cocker.

MILO: I'm just saying there's a difference between writing and real life, that's all. And there's another thing. How do I know this thing isn't one big frame-up?

ANDREW: Frame-up?

MILO: Yes. That you really hate my association with your wife, and would give five years of Olympian sexual athleticism to see me in jail. Once I'm clear of the house, an anonymous phone call to the police . . .

ANDREW: And be stuck with Marguerite for another bickering eternity? Bodystockings on the breakfast tray, false eyelashes in the washbasin, the bottles, the lotions, the unguents, the oils, the tribal record player and that ceaseless vapid yak. Oh yes, I could shop you to the police, nothing easier, but whatever for. Still, it's for you to evaluate, old boy.

MILO: Well, I . . . I, er . . .

ANDREW: If you don't trust me . . .

MILO: Oh, I trust you, but . . .

ANDREW: It's a very simple proposition. You have an expensive woman and no money. It seems to me if you want to keep Marguerite, there is only one thing you can do—you must steal those jewels.

MILO: Why don't *you* steal them and simply hand them over to me?

ANDREW: I should have thought that was obvious. The burglary has to look real. The house has actually to be broken into.

MILO: Well, why don't *you* break into it?

ANDREW: [*Brooklyn accent*] Hey, Milo baby, will you do me a favor. Leave this to me, huh? You know what I mean? Crime is my specialty. I've got such a great plan and I've got it all worked out to the last detail. You're the star, I'm just the producer.

MILO: Ninety-thousand pounds?

ANDREW: Ninety-thousand pounds tax free. In cash. It would take a lot of Tindle Tours to make that kind of money.

MILO: All right, I'll do it. Where shall I break in? [*He rushes for the stairs*]

ANDREW: Hold your horses. Now the first thing you've got to do is disguise yourself.

MILO: What on earth for?

ANDREW: Supposing someone saw you climbing in?

MILO: Who? You're not overlooked.

ANDREW: Who knows? A dallying couple. A passing sheep rapist. And, dear boy, remember the clues we're to leave for the police and the insurance company. We don't want your footsteps in the flower beds, or your coat button snagged on the window sill. Oh no, you must be disguised.

MILO: All right, what do you suggest?

ANDREW: [*He crosses to corridor and brings back a large hamper*] As Marguerite has assuredly told you, in younger days we were always dressing up in this house. What with amateur dramatics and masquerades and costume balls, there was virtually no end to the concealment of identity.

MILO: She's never mentioned it.

ANDREW: No . . . ? [*A touch wistful*] Well, it was all some years ago. [*Briskly*] Anyway, let's see what we've got. [*He opens basket and holds up the pieces of the burglar suit, one by one*] Item. A face mask, a flat cap, a striped jersey and bag marked Loot.

MILO: I thought the idea was that I was *not* to be taken as a burglar.

ANDREW: Fashions have changed, you know.

MILO: Not quickly enough. It's asking for trouble.

[ANDREW *puts the costume back and brings out a Ku Klux Klan outfit*]

ANDREW: Ku Klux Klan invade country home. Fiery cross, flames on Salisbury plain. Police baffled.

MILO: Isn't it a trifle conspicuous for Wiltshire?

ANDREW: Yes, you may be right! [*He holds up a monk's costume*] Here is one of my favorites. How about Brother Lightfingers?

MILO: Oh, for God's sake . . . [*He shakes his head decisively*]

ANDREW: Oh, come on. Let's make this a Gothic folly. [*Edgar Lustgarten voice*] Perhaps we shall never know the identity of the cowled figure seen haunting the grounds of the Manor House on the night of the terrible murder. Even today, some locals claim to hear the agonized screams of the victim echoing around the chimney pots.

MILO: Murder? Anguished screams of the victim? What are you talking about? It's a simple robbery we're staging here, that's all.

[*An uneasy pause*]

ANDREW: [*Normal voice*] Quite right, Milo. I was carried away for a moment. I'm not sure I wasn't going to add a crucified countess entombed in her bedroom, guarded by a man-eating sparrow hawk.

MILO: Look here, Andrew, you probably think this is one huge joke. But it's my freedom you're playing with.

ANDREW: I'm merely trying to bring a little romance into modern crime, and incidentally into your life.

MILO: Marguerite will bring all the romance into my life I need, thank you all the same.

ANDREW: Marguerite romantic? Marguerite couldn't have got Johann Strauss to waltz.

MILO: Look, Andrew, these are great costumes, but haven't you just got an old pair of wellies, a raincoat, and a sock that I can pull over my head?

ANDREW: Old pair of wellies and a sock? How dreary! That's the whole trouble with crime today. No imagination. I mean, you tell me, does your heart beat any faster when you hear that a truck load of cigarettes has been knocked off in the Walworth Road?

MILO: Not particularly.

ANDREW: Well of course not. Or that a ninety-three-year-old night watchman has had his silly interfering old skull split open with a lead pipe?

MILO: Of course not.

ANDREW: Well, then, what's the matter with you? Where's your spunk? Let's give our crime the true sparkle of the thirties, a little amateur aristocratic quirkiness. Think of all that wonderful material. There's the ice dagger, the poison that leaves no trace, the Regie cigarette stubbed in the ash tray, charred violet notepaper in the grate, Dusenberg tire marks in the driveway, the gramophone record simulating conversation, the clutching hand from behind the arras, sinister Orientals, twin brothers from Australia—"Hi there, cobber, hi there, blue" —where were you on the night of the thirteenth? I swear I didn't do it, Inspector, I'm innocent I tell you, innocent . . .

MILO: God, you've gone off like a firecracker!

ANDREW: And why not? We're on the brink of a great crime. Don't you feel the need to give your old arch-enemy Inspector Plodder of the Yard a run for his money? And you're the star, you're the who-what-dun-it!

MILO: Well what about this? [*He holds up courtier's costume*]

ANDREW: Ah! Monsieur Beaucaire. He's very good. Lots of beauty spots and wig powder to let fall all over the place. Or what about this? Little Bo Peep?

30

[ANDREW *sings Little Bo Peep and dances about holding up the costume*]

MILO: No.

ANDREW: Why not?

MILO: I haven't got the figure for it.

ANDREW: Are you quite sure? An indifferent figure shouldn't materially affect the execution of this crime.

MILO: Quite sure.

ANDREW: Well, you are choosy, aren't you? There's not a great deal left. [*He pulls out a clown's costume. Large pantaloons, waiter's dicky, tail coat*] We'll have to settle for "Joey."

MILO: Wow!

ANDREW: Can't you see it all, the tinsel, the glitter, the lights, the liberty horses, the roar of the crowd, and Milo all the kiddies love you.

MILO: [*Happily*] All right! It seems the costume most appropriate to this scheme.

ANDREW: Well, give me your coat. I'll hang it up for you. We don't want the police to find any fibers of

31

this beautiful suit. [MILO *takes off his jacket and gives it to* ANDREW] Oh, and the shirt and trousers too.

MILO: What?

ANDREW: Oh, yes, you know how clever they are in those laboratories of theirs. That's it. Don't be shy. Into your smalls. Oh, I know a well-brought-up boy when I see one. Folds his pants at night.

> [MILO *gives him his carefully folded trousers.* ANDREW *runs up the stairs, and with a sudden violent gesture, roughly throws the suit into the wardrobe, while* MILO *takes off his shirt and tie and shoes*]

MILO: Shirt and shoes. [MILO *holds up his shirt, shoes and tie*]

ANDREW: Very good, sir. The Quick Clean Valet Service always at your disposal, sir. [*He pushes them into the wardrobe, then watches* MILO *changing with great satisfaction. Softly*] Give a clown your finger and he'll take your hand.

MILO: What was that?

ANDREW: Just an old English proverb I was thinking of.

[MILO *sings to himself "On With The Mot-ley" and ends it with "Ninety-thousand pounds tax free, in cash" as he dresses*]

MILO: Ecco, Milo!

ANDREW: Bravissimo! Now all you need are the boots.

[MILO *pulls a huge pair of boots from the basket*]

MILO: Hey, I could go skiing on these when I go to Italy.

ANDREW:
"The clown is such a happy chap,
His nose is painted red,
His trousers baggy as can be,
A topper on his head.
He jumps around the circus ring,
And juggles for his bread,
Then comes the day he tries a trick,
And drops down . . ."
Come on do us a trick.

MILO: What sort of trick?

ANDREW: Oh, I don't know. Trip up—fall on your arse.

MILO: Certainly not, I don't think that's a very good idea.

ANDREW: Well, what about a bit of juggling then.

[ANDREW *takes two oranges from the drinks table and throws them to* MILO. *He then produces an umbrella from the basket and throws it to* MILO *who opens it and runs about the room and finally trips up on his boots*]

MILO: Christ!

ANDREW: Sorry, dear boy. But you know the rule of the circus. If at first you don't succeed . . .

MILO: Give up. Can we get on with this charade, please!

ANDREW: Of course. Yours to command. [*He opens swag bag*] Here are the tools of your trade. One glass cutter to break in with; a piece of putty for holding on to the cut piece of glass so it doesn't clatter onto the floor and awake the ravenous Doberman pinscher you suspect lurks inside; and a stethoscope.

MILO: A stethoscope?

ANDREW: Safe breakers for the use of. The theory is you tried to pick the lock by listening to the tumblers, failed, and then employed gelignite.

MILO: [*Alarmed*] Gelignite?

ANDREW: Yes. Leave that to me. Now how about some bizarre touch—say a signed photograph of Grock left impaled on a splinter of glass.

MILO: A signed photograph of Grock. [*Angry*] Why don't you take a full page ad in *The Times* and tell them what we're doing.

ANDREW: I was only trying to lighten Inspector Plodder's day for him . . . If you don't like the idea . . .

MILO: [*Earnestly*] There's no such animal as Inspector Plodder outside of books. It'll be Inspector Early Bird, or Superintendent No Stone Unturned. You can bet your bottom dollar on that and I can't walk in this costume. These boots are ridiculous. [*He stumbles and starts to take them off*]

ANDREW: Keep them on. Can't you see it all. Wiltshire paralyzed. The West Country in a ferment. Where will Big Boot strike next?

MILO: But . . .

ANDREW: [*Reasonably*] All these boots will tell the

police is that a true professional realized the flower beds would carry footprints, and decided to disguise his own perhaps a trifle eccentrically. Now are you ready? Got everything? Glass cutter? Putty?

ANDREW:
MILO: } The mask!

[ANDREW *takes top hat and mask from basket.* MILO *puts them on*]

ANDREW: Good. Now go through that door, round the house and across the lawn. To your right you will discover a shed. In it is a ladder. Bring the ladder back and stand it against the house so you can break in at the gallery.

MILO: Will you come out and hold it steady?

ANDREW: Certainly not. I don't want *my* footprints in the flowerbeds.

MILO: I'm not very good at heights.

ANDREW: Improvise. Place one foot above the other. It's called climbing.

MILO: OK.

ANDREW: Good luck.

[MILO *bows and goes through the hall door.*
ANDREW *takes a length of flex and black box
with gelignite, black tape and detonator
from desk drawer. After a few minutes* MILO
appears at window]

ANDREW: For Christ's sake can't you keep those bloody
boots off my Busy Lizzies. [MILO *disappears and
presently reappears with the ladder which he places
against the window and starts to climb.* ANDREW
*sits with his back to the window and reacts to the
noises he hears. As he attaches the detonator to the
flex he speaks in an old woman's voice*] Puss, Puss,
Puss, do you hear a noise, Puss! Was that a step on
the stairs. No, it was just the wind. You know, Puss,
I sometimes think there's a curse on this house. But
you shouldn't pay any attention to me. I'm just a
silly old woman who is afraid of her own shadow.
[*Noise of glass cutter scoring window*] What was
that, Puss? Someone's prowling in the grounds.
We're all going to be murdered in our beds. No, no,
the front door's locked, and the window's too high,
no one can get into our snug little home.

[MILO *drops pane of glass*]

ANDREW: [*Exasperated*] What *are* you doing now?

MILO: I dropped the glass. [ANDREW *groans theatrically. After a further struggle,* MILO *succeeds in climbing in through the window, onto the gallery*] Whew! What do I do with the putty? [*He indicates the putty*]

ANDREW: Stick it on the wall.

MILO: I can lose this at any rate. [*He puts mask on bureau*] Now for the safe!

ANDREW: No. Not straight away. You're not meant to know where they are. Search around. Go into the bedroom. Disturb a few things. Throw some clothes on the floor—Marguerite's for choice . . . That's it.

> [MILO *goes into the bedroom and returns with a pile of women's clothes which he puts neatly on the floor*]

ANDREW: [*Rushes up to gallery*] Don't pack 'em. Ravage 'em. Don't you know how burglars leave a place? [*He takes a flying kick at the pile of his wife's clothes—sending them flying all over the room*] Now try the wardrobe. Rumple the contents a little. Actually that's enough. Those shirts were made for me by Baget and Grub, chemise makers to monarchs.

MILO: [*Throws the shirts out with relish*] Got to be thorough. It would be suspicious if the burglar played favorites.

[ANDREW's *socks and underwear follow, cascading out all over the gallery*]

ANDREW: Oh, it's a martyrdom. [*Shouting*] Will you stop that, Milo, and rifle that bureau immediately.

[*Reluctantly* MILO *crosses to the bureau and tries a drawer*]

MILO: It's locked.

ANDREW: Of course it's bloody locked! Use your jimmy on it.

MILO: I haven't got a jimmy. You didn't give me one.

ANDREW: [*Exasperated*] Well, we'd better go and find one, hadn't we? [*They tramp downstairs*] Honestly, Milo, you are the soppiest night interloper I've ever met. I can't think what Marguerite sees in you.

MILO: The sympathy and kindness of a kindred spirit, actually.

ANDREW: It's like a Bengali tiger lying down with a
bush baby.

MILO: I know we're a damn sight happier than you
are with your ice maiden.

ANDREW: You probably take it more seriously, that's
all.

MILO: You have to be serious if you want to be in
love.

ANDREW: You have to be serious about crime if you
want to afford to be in love. Now get cracking on
that bureau.

> [MILO *climbs the stairs. He starts work on
> the bureau with the jimmy. After a pause
> the drawer yields and he opens it*]

MILO: There is a set of false teeth. They look like a
man's.

ANDREW: [*Furious*] Put them back at once.

MILO: Sorry. Your spares?

ANDREW: [*Pause*] Come down at once. [MILO *comes
down the stairs and crosses to* ANDREW *who has
plugged the flex into a light switch*] Keep your feet

off the flex. Right, stand by for count down five—
four—three—two—one. Contact!

> [*Noise of explosion and puff of smoke from
> safe*]

MILO: There she blows. Ah! It's hot.

ANDREW: You've got gloves on! Get in there! [MILO
*rummages in the safe and finds a large jewel box.
He examines it carefully, occasionally shaking it
gently*] What the hell are you shaking it for? It's
a jewel box, not a maraca.

MILO: I thought it might have some secret catch on
it. It's locked, you see.

ANDREW: Well, smash it open. Jesus! You've all the
killer instinct of a twenty-year-old Sealyham.

> [MILO *attacks the box with his jimmy*]

MILO: It's such a pretty box—it seems such a waste.
[*The box opens to reveal its precious contents.* MILO
*stands entranced, letting the jewels flash and sparkle
through his fingers*] Dear God!

ANDREW: Ah! Moses looks upon the promised land.

MILO: [*Sits at base of stairs*] They're very beautiful. Look at this ruby necklace?

ANDREW: That we got on our honeymoon.

MILO: It's fantastic.

ANDREW: I never cared for it myself. I always thought it made Marguerite look like a blood sacrifice.

MILO: I'd like my father to be here now. Poor blighter, he had no idea what it was all about . . . sitting there every night, hunched up over those watches like a little old gnome, squinting his eyesight away, and for what—to give me an education at a second-rate prep school. I suppose he thought he had to do it—that he owed it to me and the brave new Anglo-Saxon world he'd adopted. Poor old bugger.

ANDREW: Here, put them in your pocket for a start. I'll get you the receipts in a moment. Now! This is the fun bit. It's the moment when the householder, his attention attracted by the noise of the explosion, surprises his burglar. In the ensuing struggle, the house is sacked.

MILO: Why is it necessary for you to surprise me at all?

ANDREW: Because if I've seen you at close quarters, I can always describe you to the police . . .

[MILO *reacts as if hit*]

MILO: Now look here . . .

ANDREW: . . . wrongly. [INSPECTOR's *voice*] Did you manage to get a good look at the intruder's face, sir? [*Normal voice*] Yes, Inspector, I did. It may just have been a trick of the light, but his face didn't look wholly human. If you can imagine a kind of prognathic stoat, fringed about with lilac-colored hair, and seemingly covered with a sort of boot polish . . .

MILO: [*Patiently*] I understand. How much sacking do you want done?

ANDREW: A decent bit, I think, a few chairs on their backs, some china ornaments put to the sword. You know—convincing but not Carthaginian. [MILO *carefully turns a chair over and leans a small table against the sofa. He takes a china ornament and stands it upright on the floor.* ANDREW *watches impatiently*] Surely you don't call that convincing? [ANDREW *throws over another table, spills the con-*

tents of a drawer, and turns books out of his book-case] That's better. Let the encyclopedias fly like autumn leaves. [MILO *throws papers in the air*] We'll let my assistant sort that lot out. You know I never liked Saltglaze. [*He drops a china ornament to the floor where it breaks*] I can't think why Marguerite is devoted to it. [*The two men survey the room*] It still doesn't look right. Come on. Let's see what accident does to artifice.

[ANDREW *seizes* MILO *and wrestles him round the room, overturning things as they go.* MILO, *apart from being the shorter, is much hampered by his big boots and floppy clown's clothing, so that* ANDREW *is able to pummel him severely*]

MILO: You're bigger than I am. It's not fair.

ANDREW: Nonsense. You're the underdog, aren't you? You've got the support of the crowd.

MILO: A good big 'un will always lick a good little 'un.

ANDREW: The bigger they are the harder they fall.

[MILO *receives a particularly hard blow*]

44

MILO: Here, steady on, old man!

ANDREW: They never come back. [*He pushes* MILO *over the fender into the fireplace*]

MILO: Christ! That hurt!

[ANDREW *helps him up*]

ANDREW: Come on, back into the ring. Don't despair. This fight is fixed. It's about now that I take a dive. This is where you lay me out cold.

MILO: What? For real?

ANDREW: Naturally. When the police come I must be able to show them a real bump. [MILO *smiles weakly*] I thought you'd like this bit.

MILO: [*Tentatively moving towards a lamp*] What shall I use?

ANDREW: Not my opaline if you don't mind.

MILO: [*Picks up the brass poker*] This is it. The poker, the original blunt instrument. [*He beats logs viciously*]

ANDREW: [*Eyes the poker apprehensively*] Steady on, Milo. Don't get carried away.

MILO: Well, I'm doing my best.

ANDREW: We are not talking about a murder weapon. We are discussing an object from which I receive, in the classic formula, a glancing blow which renders me temporarily unconscious.

MILO: Such as?

ANDREW: Well I don't know exactly. Why don't you use your imagination? Ask yourself what those fathers of the scientific detective story—R. Austin Freeman or Arthur B. Reeve—would have come up with.

MILO: Huh?

ANDREW: You know—"The Red Thumb Mark," 1907. "The Silent Bullet," 1912. [MILO *still looks blank*] Oh, do try . . . I know, perhaps we could think of a device which will raise a lump but not damage the cranium.

MILO: [*Trapped into joining in*] How about a bee sting projected into the scalp with a blowpipe?

ANDREW: Do you have such sting, pipe or bee?

MILO: Well . . . no.

ANDREW: No. Still seven out of ten for trying. I know,

you can always tie me up and gag me and leave me to be found by the cleaning woman. [*Charlady's voice*]: Lawks, Mr. Wyke, what are doing all trussed up like a turkey cock? [*He mimes being tied up and gaged and trying to get the Charlady to untie him*] Mmmmmmmmmmmmm . . . Mmmmmmmmmm mm . . . Mmmmmmmmmmmm . . . [*Charlady's voice*]: Trying out something for one of them creepy books of yours, are you, sir? Well, don't mind me. I won't disturb you. I'll just get on with the dusting.

MILO: [*Patiently*] If I don't knock you out, how do I manage to tie you up?

ANDREW: [*Normal voice*] That's a very good question. I know. You could hold a gun on me.

MILO: We professional burglars don't like firearms much.

ANDREW: But, as you're a rank amateur, you can conquer your scruples. [*He produces a gun from the desk drawer*] Here. How about this? Don't you think its wicked-looking blue barrel is just the thing.

MILO: Is it loaded?

ANDREW: Naturally. What use would it be otherwise?

Perhaps it should go off in the struggle.

MILO: Why?

ANDREW: It would add credence to my story of your holding a gun on me. Hearing a noise and fearing burglars, I took my revolver and went to investigate. You attacked me. In the struggle it went off, blowing to smithereens several priceless heirlooms. Being an old fraidy cat householder, I allowed brutish you to take possession of it. You then held it on me while you tied me up. Right?

MILO: I suppose so.

ANDREW: Uninventive but believable. Now then, what to sacrifice? What do you say to the demolition of that gaudy Swansea puzzle jug? The gloriously witty idea is that when you tip it up the liquid pours out of a hole in the back, and not through the spout.

MILO: A bit obvious, really.

ANDREW: Exactly! Obvious and ugly. Let us expose its shortcomings. [*He draws a bead on it, then lowers the gun*] On the other hand, the crème brulé coloring lends it an attractive solidity I should miss. Now how about that giant Staffordshire mug with the inscription on it? What does it say?

MILO: [*Moves a little toward it and reads aloud*] "In the real cabinet of friendship everyone helped his neighbor and said to his brother, be of good cheer."

ANDREW: Proletarian pomposity! [*He suddenly raises his gun and fires, shattering the jug. MILO turns in surprise, as he realizes the bullet must have passed reasonably close to his head*] You might have said good shot.

MILO: Good shot.

ANDREW: [*Insouciant*] It's nothing. [*He looks around him. His eye falls on a china figurine poised on the banister rail above him. He takes aim*] Down with all imperialistic, deviationist, reactionary Dresden shepherdesses. [*He shoots and the Dresden shepherdess flies into pieces*]

MILO: Bravo!

ANDREW: What fun this is! Did you ever know Charlie Begby?

MILO: I don't think so.

ANDREW: Terribly funny fellow. I once saw him bag three brace of duck with one shot. The only trouble was they were china ducks on his auntie's drawing room wall. I said, "Oh Charlie, you can't do that, it's the closed season." [*He presses button on desk and the sailor laughs*] I told you he always laughs at my jokes. [MILO *laughs.* ANDREW'*s mood changes abruptly*] It's not really all that funny. There's an open season on some creatures all the year round. [*He turns the gun on* MILO] Seducers and wife stealers for example.

MILO: [*Nervous*] Only in Italian opera, surely.

ANDREW: [*Hard*] You should know. It's your country of origin, is it not?

MILO: No. I was actually born here in England.

ANDREW: Were you now. Dear old cradle-of-the-parliamentary-system-who-screws-my-wife-merits-a-large-pink-gin-England?

MILO: Sense-of-humor-fair-trial-England, I mean.

ANDREW: That's the way a foreigner talks. In private he thinks, filthy wet country, ugly red cold men who don't know how to treat women.

MILO: What's brought all this on? What are you doing with that gun?

ANDREW: Pretty obviously pointing it at you.

MILO: For God's sake, why?

ANDREW: [*Slowly, Italian accent*] Because I'm going to kill you.

MILO: You're going to . . . [*Laughs nervously*] Oh Jesus! I suppose this is some sort of game.

ANDREW: Yes. We've been playing it all evening. It's called "You're going to die and no-one will suspect murder."

[*A pause.* MILO *considers his position*]

MILO: You mean all this steal-my-wife's-jewels stuff was just a . . .

ANDREW: Of course! I invited you here to set up the circumstances of your own death. The break in, the disguise, the jewels in your pocket, the householder aroused, the gun going off in the struggle and then the final fatal shot. I might even get a commendation from the police, for "having a go."

MILO: For God's sake, Andrew, knock it off!

ANDREW: Can you find a flaw in it?

MILO: [*Beginning to feel desperate*] Marguerite! They'll trace the connection between me and Marguerite. They'll know that's why you did it.

ANDREW: I am quite entitled to tackle a man wearing a mask, plundering my house in the middle of the night. How was I expected to know who you were. Oh no, the law will have every sympathy with me. Property has always been more highly regarded than people in England. Even Marguerite will assume you were just an adventurer who only loved her for her jewels—a petty sneak thief who found larceny less burdensome than marriage. You really are a dead duck, aren't you? Not a moral or romantic attitude left.

MILO: I believe you *are* serious.

ANDREW: I'm not afraid of killing you, if that's what you mean.

MILO: You've got to be. Mortally afraid for your soul.

ANDREW: I didn't think the Jews believed in hell.

MILO: We believe in not playing games with life.

ANDREW: Ha! Wit in the face of adversity. You've learnt something from the English. All right, here's another thing. A sporting chance. Why don't you make a run for it?

MILO: And give you the chance to shoot me down in cold blood?

ANDREW: Hot blood, you mean. I'm going to shoot you down in cold blood anyway.

[MILO *tries to run but falls over his boots*]

MILO: Look, stop pointing that gun at me . . . I hate guns . . . please . . . this is sick.

ANDREW: You should be flattered by the honor I'm doing you—to take your life light-heartedly—to make your death the center piece of an arranged bit of fun. To put it another way, your demise will recreate a noble mind.

MILO: This is where I came in.

ANDREW: And where you go out, I'm afraid. The only question to be decided is where the police shall find you. Sprawled over the desk like countless colonels in countless studies? Or propped up in the log basket like a rag doll? Which do you think? Early Agatha Christie or middle S. S. Van Dine?

MILO: For Christ's sake, Andrew, this is not a detective story, this is real life. You are talking of doing a real murder. Of killing a real man—don't you understand?

ANDREW: Perhaps I shouldn't do it with a gun at all.

Perhaps I should shove the ham knife into you, and leave you face down in the middle of the room— [*Melodramatic voice*]—your blood staining the flagstones a deep carmine.

MILO: [*Shudders*] Oh God!

ANDREW: Or best of all, how about a real 1930's murder weapon—the mashie niblick. I've got one in my golf bag. [*He fetches the golf club from the hall. MILO dives for the telephone but is too late*] You would be discovered in the fireplace, I think, in a fair old mess. [*Dramatic voice*] The body lay on its back, its limbs grotesquely splayed like a broken puppet. The whole head had been pulped as if by some superhuman force. "My God," breathed the Inspector, blanching. "Thompson, you'd better get a tarpaulin . . . Excuse me, sir, but was all this violence strictly necessary?" "I'm sorry, Inspector. It was when I saw him handling my wife's nightdresses. I must have completely lost control of myself." [ANDREW *throws down the golf club*] No. I think the scene the police find is simply this. After the fight you flee up the stairs, back to your ladder. I catch you on the landing and in the renewed struggle I shoot you. Nothing succeeds like simplicity, don't you agree, Milo? Now then, some of my own fingerprints on my own revolver. [*He takes his glove off and holds the gun in his naked hand*] On your feet, up! [ANDREW *forces* MILO *to mount the stairs by shoving the gun in his back.* MILO *gives a sudden spasmodic shudder*] Did you know that Charles I put on two shirts the morning of his execution? "If I tremble with cold," he said, "my enemies will say it was from fear; I will not expose myself to such reproaches." You must also attempt dignity as you mount the steps to the scaffold.

[MILO *demurs and sinks to his knees near the top step*]

MILO: [*Terrified and pleading*] But why, Andrew? Why?

ANDREW: Don't snivel. You can't think it'll gain you mercy.

MILO: I must know why!

ANDREW: I'm amazed you have to ask. But since you do, it's perfectly simple. I hate you. I hate your smarmy, good-looking Latin face and your easy manner. I'll bet you're easy in a ski lodge, and easy on a yacht, and easy on a beach. I'll bet you a pound to a penny that you wear a gold charm round your neck, and that your chest is hairy and in summer matted with sun oil. I hate you because you are a mock humble, jeweled, shot cufflinked sponger, a world is my oyster-er, a seducer of silly women, and a king among marshmallow snakes. I hate you because you are a culling spick. A wop—a not one-of-me. Come, little man, did you really believe I would give up my wife and jewels to you? That I would make myself *that* ridiculous.

MILO: Why not? You're not in love with her.

ANDREW: She's mine whether I love her or not. I found her, I've kept her. I am familiar with her. And once, she was in love with me.

MILO: And now she's in love with me, and the dog in the manger won't let go. [*He tries to attack him*] The mad dog in the manger who should be put down for everyone's sake.

ANDREW: [*Deadly*] And you are a young man, dressed as a clown about to be murdered. Put the mask on, Milo. [*A pause*]

MILO: No, please.

[ANDREW *reaches up and lifts the clown mask*

off the banister where MILO *had previously hung it*]

ANDREW: Put it on! [MILO *takes the mask and fumbles it onto his face*] Excellent. Farewell, Punchinello!

[ANDREW *lifts the pistol to* MILO's *head.* MILO *is shaking with fear*]

MILO: [*High falsetto*] Please ...

[ANDREW *slowly pulls the trigger.* MILO *falls backwards down the stairs and lies still.* ANDREW *walks past him, pausing to peer closely to see whether there is any sign of life. He lifts the lolling head and lets it thump back, carelessly, onto the stairs. Satisfied that he has done his work well, he straightens up, and smiles to himself*]

ANDREW: Game and set, I believe.

SLOW CURTAIN

ACT TWO

Two days later.

*The curtain rises to the sound of the slow move-
ment of Beethoven's Seventh Symphony which is
playing on a record player.* ANDREW *enters from
kitchen with a tray containing a large pot of caviare,
toast, wedge of lemon, a bottle of champagne and
glass. He puts tray on desk and stands conducting the
music. The movement comes to an end.* ANDREW
*crosses to record player and turns over the record. He
returns to desk and starts to eat. The telephone rings.*

ANDREW: Hullo . . . Yes, Hawkins, where are you?
What? Well you should have checked the times of
the trains . . . I've had to get my own supper for
the third time running . . . Yes, yes, I daresay, but
you know how helpless I am without you and Mrs.
H. Man cannot live by baked beans alone, you
know . . . All right . . . All right, tomorrow morning.
But the first thing, mind you.

[ANDREW *continues eating for some minutes. The front doorbell rings. After a slight pause* ANDREW *goes to answer it*]

DOPPLER: [*Offstage, in hall*] Good evening, sir.

ANDREW: [*Offstage*] Evening.

DOPPLER: Mr. Wyke.

ANDREW: Yes.

DOPPLER: My name is Inspector Doppler, sir. Detective Inspector Doppler. Of the Wiltshire County Constabulary. I'm sorry to be calling so late. May I have a few words with you on a very important matter?

[ANDREW *enters, followed by* INSPECTOR DOPPLER, *a heavily built, tallish man of about fifty. His hair is balding, and he wears cheap, round spectacles on his fleshy nose, above a greying moustache. His clothes—dark rumpled suit, under a half-open light-colored mackintosh—occasion no surprise, nor does his porkpie hat*]

ANDREW: The Wiltshire County Constabulary you

say? [*Turning off music*] Come in. Always pleased
to see the police.

DOPPLER: Can't say the same about everyone, sir. Most
people seem to have what you might call an allergy
to us.

ANDREW: Would you join me in a brandy, Inspector?
Or are you going to tell me you don't drink on duty?

DOPPLER: Oh, no, sir. I always drink on duty. I can't
afford to in my own time. [*He sits down*]

ANDREW: [*Handing the* INSPECTOR *a brandy*] Well,
what can I do for you, Inspector?

DOPPLER: I'm investigating a disappearance, sir.

ANDREW: Disappearance?

DOPPLER: Yes, sir. Of a Mr. Milo Tindle. Do you
know him, sir?

ANDREW: Yes, that's the chap who's taken Laundry
Cottage.

DOPPLER: He walked out of his cottage on Friday
night and hasn't been seen since.

ANDREW: Great Scott!

DOPPLER: Do you know this gentleman well, sir?

ANDREW: Vaguely. He came to the house once or twice. How can I help you?

DOPPLER: When did you last see Mr. Tindle, sir?

ANDREW: Oh, months ago. I can't exactly remember. As I told you, he wasn't a close friend; rather more an acquaintance.

DOPPLER: Really, sir? That doesn't quite accord with our information. In fact, he told Jack Benn, the licensee of the White Lion, he was coming to see you, two nights ago.

ANDREW: Barmen are notorious opponents of exactitude, Inspector. Vinous gossip is their stock in trade. In particular, I've always found that Jack Benn's observations need constant correction.

DOPPLER: Really, sir? I was wondering if you could correct something else for me.

ANDREW: What's that?

DOPPLER: The impression gained by a man who happened to be passing your house two nights ago, that a fierce struggle was taking place in here.

ANDREW: Does it look like it?

DOPPLER: And that shots were fired?

ANDREW: [*Uncertainly*] Shots?

DOPPLER: Three, our man thinks.

ANDREW: A car backfiring?

DOPPLER: No, sir. These were shots. From a gun. Our man is positive.

ANDREW: May I ask why you took two days to call round and ask me about all this?

DOPPLER: Well, sir, things take longer to check out than you think. We like to be certain of our facts before troubling a gentleman like yourself.

ANDREW: Facts? What facts?

DOPPLER: After our informant reported the incident, we did a spot of checking in the village, and as I say, Mr. Benn was very helpful.

ANDREW: There's an upright citizen, then.

DOPPLER: Quite so, sir.

ANDREW: If there were more like him . . .

DOPPLER: He told us that Mr. Tindle popped into the pub Friday evening for a quick one, and said he was just on his way up to you. Well, what with him

being a newcomer to these parts and all, we thought
we'd better have a word with him, and see if he
could throw any light on the subject. But as I previously indicated, he seems to have disappeared, sir.

ANDREW: But what's that got to do with me?

DOPPLER: He wasn't at his cottage all of Saturday, nor
all today. We must have called half a dozen times.

ANDREW: By Jove, Merridew would have been proud
of you. Now Inspector, if that's all you have to
say . . .

DOPPLER: When we stepped inside Mr. Tindle's cottage to make sure he'd come to no harm, we found
this note, sir. [*Reading*] "Urgent we talk. Come
Friday night eight o'clock. Wyke." May I ask
whether this is your handwriting, sir?

[DOPPLER *shows him the note.* ANDREW *tries
to retain it, but* DOPPLER *takes it back*]

ANDREW: [*Trapped*] Yes. It's mine all right.

DOPPLER: So Mr. Tindle *was* here?

ANDREW: Yes. The Potman spoke sooth.

DOPPLER: Perhaps you wouldn't mind answering my original question now, sir.

ANDREW: Which one?

DOPPLER: Was there a struggle here two nights ago?

ANDREW: In a manner of speaking, yes. It was a game we were playing.

DOPPLER: A game? What kind of game?

ANDREW: It's rather difficult to explain. It's called Burglary.

DOPPLER: Please don't joke, sir.

ANDREW: Isn't it about time you told me I don't know the seriousness of my own position?

DOPPLER: A man comes here, there is a fight. Shots are heard. He disappears. What would you make of that if you were me?

ANDREW: An open and shut case. But things are not always what they seem, Inspector. In "The Case of the Drowned Dummy" my man, Merridew, once proved by a phonetic misspelling the forgery of a document allegedly written by a deaf mute.

DOPPLER: I'm waiting for an explanation, sir.

ANDREW: Tindle arrived at eight and left about an hour and a half later. I haven't seen him since.

DOPPLER: And nor has anyone else, sir.

ANDREW: This is absurd. Are you suggesting that I killed Tindle?

DOPPLER: Killed Tindle, sir. I never mentioned kill.

ANDREW: Oh really! You can't pull that old one on me. [*Mimicking* INSPECTOR's *voice*]: Garotted, sir? Might I ask how you knew that her ladyship was garotted? [*Normal voice*]: Surely *you* told me so, Inspector. [*Inspector's voice*]: No, sir. I never mentioned it.

DOPPLER: I'm sorry you find us so comic, sir. On the whole what we do is necessary.

ANDREW: "You're just doing your job," that's the overworked phrase, isn't it?

DOPPLER: Possibly, sir. Your wife and Mr. Tindle have been associating closely for some time.

ANDREW: Oh, so you know about that, do you? I suppose you can't keep anything quiet in a small village.

DOPPLER: Perfectly true, sir.

ANDREW: You aren't suggesting a crime passionel, I hope, Inspector—not over Marguerite. It would be like knifing somebody for a tablespoonful of Co-operative white blancmange.

DOPPLER: I'm very partial to blancmange, sir. I find it a great standby.

ANDREW: [*Oratorically*] "All of you had either means, motive or opportunity," said Inspector Doppler as he thoughtfully digested another spoonful of his favorite pud. "But only one of you had all three."

DOPPLER: Exactly so, sir! That person is you.

ANDREW: Forgive me, Inspector. I suppose I'd better tell you what happened.

DOPPLER: Yes.

ANDREW: Want a bribe to believe it?

DOPPLER: I'll have another drink.

ANDREW: As you seem to know, Tindle was having an affair with my wife. Now, I'm one of that rare breed of men who genuinely don't mind losing gracefully to a gent who's playing by the same rules. But to be worsted by a flash crypto Italian lover, who mistakes my boredom for impotence and my provoca-

67

tive energy for narcissism is too much. It's like start-
ing every game—thirty down, and the umpire
against you.

DOPPLER: You mean you couldn't bring yourself to
accept the situation, sir. Is that what you're saying?

ANDREW: I think what infuriated me most was the
things he said about me—things that Marguerite
repeated to me. I mean, no man likes to listen to
the other man's witticisms when he's trying to
choke down his late night Ovaltine.

DOPPLER: What sort of things, sir?

ANDREW: Oh you know, smarmy, deceitful things
which any lover can make about any husband. It's
just too easy for them with a captive audience
groggy on rediscovered youth and penis envy.
[*Pause*] It's not really playing the game.

DOPPLER: You seem to regard marriage as a game, sir.

ANDREW: Not marriage, Inspector. *Sex*. Sex is the
game with marriage the penalty. Round the board
we jog towards each futile anniversary. Pass go.
Collect two hundred rows, two hundred silences,
two hundred scars in the deep places. It's just as

well that I don't lack for amorous adventure. Finlandia provides.

DOPPLER: Are you trying to tell me that because of your indifference to your wife, you had no motive for killing Mr. Tindle?

ANDREW: I'm simply saying that in common with most men I want to have my cookie and ignore it. That's rather witty!

DOPPLER: Well, sir. I must say you're very frank.

ANDREW: Disarmingly so, I hope.

DOPPLER: Please go on.

ANDREW: As I say. I thought I'd teach Mr. Tindle a lesson for his presumption. In a curious way, some of his remarks, which Marguerite repeated to me, led me to believe that he was worth taking a little trouble with—even perhaps worth getting to know. Well, the shortest way to a man's heart is humiliation. You soon find out what he's made of.

DOPPLER: So you invited him here and humiliated him?

ANDREW: I did indeed. I took a leaf out of the book of certain eighteenth-century secret societies. They

knew to a nicety how to determine whether someone was worthy to be included among their number
and also how to humiliate him in the process. I
refer of course to the initiation ceremony.

DOPPLER: Would it be something like bullying a new
boy at school?

ANDREW: Not unlike, but the victim had the choice
of refusal. When Count Cagliostro, the noted ma-
gician, sought admission to one such society, he
was asked whether he was prepared to die for it,
if need be. He said he was. He was then sentenced
to death, blindfolded and a pistol containing powder
but no shot placed against his temple and dis-
charged.

DOPPLER: And you did this to Mr. Tindle?

ANDREW: More or less. I invited Milo here and sug-
gested to him that as my wife had expensive tastes
and he was virtually a pauper, the only course open
for him was to steal some valuable jewels which I
had in the safe.

DOPPLER: And he agreed to this?

ANDREW: With alacrity. I persuaded him to get out of
his clothes and to dress as Grock, in which ludi-

crous disguise he broke into the house and blew
open the safe. He then pocketed the jewels, strug-
gled convincingly round this room and was about
to make off, when I turned nasty and revealed the
purpose of the evening. This of course was that I
had maneuvered him into a position where by pre-
tending to mistake him for a burglar, I could, as
the outraged householder, legitimately shoot him as
he raced away up the stairs. By the time the police
arrived I would be standing in my night attire, innocent, bewildered and aggrieved. And as you well
know, Inspector, there's no liar in Britain, however
unconvincing, more likely to be believed than an
owner occupier standing with his hair ruffled in
front of his own fireplace, wearing striped Viyella
pajamas under a camel Jaeger dressing gown.

DOPPLER: What was Mr. Tindle's reaction to all this?

ANDREW: It was electrifying! He swallowed my story
hook, line and sinker. He fell on his knees, and
pleaded for his life, but I was implacable. I put the
gun against his head and shot him with a *blank* cartridge. He fainted dead away. It was most gratifying.

DOPPLER: Gratifying or not, sir, Mr. Tindle must have

been put in fear for his life. Such action invites a grave charge of assault.

ANDREW: Well, I suppose that's marginally better than the murder charge you were contemplating a few minutes ago.

DOPPLER: I still am contemplating it, sir.

ANDREW: Oh come now, Inspector. I've told you what happened. After a few minutes, Mr. Tindle recovered his senses, realized shrewdly that he wasn't dead after all and went off home.

DOPPLER: [*Shaking his head in disbelief*] Just like that?

ANDREW: Well, he needed a glass or two of cognac to get the parts working. I mean, wouldn't you?

DOPPLER: I doubt whether I would have survived completely undamaged, sir. The whole thing sounds like the most irresponsible trick.

ANDREW: Irresponsible? It was quite the contrary. I was upholding the sanctity of marriage. That's more than most people are prepared to do these days. By this action I was clearly stating "Marriage isn't dead. It's alive and well and living in Wiltshire."

DOPPLER: Tell me, did Mr. Tindle say anything when he left?

ANDREW: No. He seemed speechless. [*Laughs*] He just lurched off.

DOPPLER: I'm sorry you appear to find all this so funny, Mr. Wyke. We may not take quite the same attitude.

ANDREW: Look, why don't you see this from my point of view. In a sense, Milo *was* a burglar. He was stealing my wife.

DOPPLER: So you tortured him?

ANDREW: [*Exploding*] Don't you see. It was a *game!*

DOPPLER: A game?

ANDREW: A bloody game, yes!

DOPPLER: It sounds rather sad, sir—like a child not growing up.

ANDREW: What's so sad about a child playing, eh!

DOPPLER: Nothing, sir—if you're a child.

ANDREW: Let me tell you, Inspector. I have played games of such complexity that Jung and Einstein would have been honored to have been asked to participate in them. Games of construction and games of destruction. Games of hazard, and games of callidity. Games of deductive logic, inductive logic, semantics, color association, mathematics, hypnosis and prestidigitation. I have achieved leaps of the mind and leaps of the psyche unknown in ordinary human relationships. And I've had a great deal of not wholly innocent fun.

DOPPLER: And now, sir, you have achieved murder.

ANDREW: No!

DOPPLER: I believe so, sir.

ANDREW: No!

DOPPLER: Would you mind if I looked around?

ANDREW: Go ahead. Crawl about the floor on hands and knees. Get your envelope out and imprison hairs. Gather ye blunt instruments while ye may.

[DOPPLER *rises and starts to examine the room*]

ANDREW: [*Slowly*] I ask myself, if I wanted to conceal Milo . . . [DOPPLER *shakes the sailor on his passage round the room*] . . . where would I put him? In the cellar? . . . Too traditional! In the water tank? . . . Too poisonous! In the linen chest? . . . Too aromatic! In the furnace? . . . Too residual! In the herbaceous border? . . . Too ossiferous! In the . . .

DOPPLER: Excuse me sir, but these holes in the wall here and here. They look like bullet holes.

ANDREW: [*Slowly*] Quite right, Inspector. So they are.

DOPPLER: I understood you to say, sir, that you used a blank.

ANDREW: Two live bullets to set up the trick. One blank to complete it. I had to persuade Tindle I was in earnest. After all, there's really no point in playing a game unless you play it to the hilt.

DOPPLER: I see, sir. One blank. I'd like you to show me where Mr. Tindle was when you killed him.

ANDREW: Pretended to kill him, you mean.

DOPPLER: Quite so, sir. Show me, please, exactly where he was when the bullet hit him.

ANDREW: You do realize, of course, there wasn't a real bullet.

DOPPLER: [*Skeptically*] Very well, sir. Show me where he was when the blank cartridge was fired.

[ANDREW *mounts the stairs, followed by the Inspector*]

ANDREW: He was standing, kneeling, crouching about here. He fainted and fell down the stairs. Bang!

[DOPPLER *passes* ANDREW]

DOPPLER: I see. About here you say, sir?

ANDREW: Towards me. Come on. Come on. Stop.

DOPPLER: Were you close to Mr. Tindle when you fired the gun?

ANDREW: Very. I was standing over him, in fact, with the gun pressed against his head. The actual feel of the gun coupled with the noise of the explosion was what did the trick. [DOPPLER *scrutinizes the staircase*] Could I interest you in a magnifying glass?

[DOPPLER *bends down to examine the staircase, then the banisters. Suddenly he rubs a finger on them, and straightens up, wiping them on his handkerchief*]

DOPPLER: Joke blood, sir?

ANDREW: [*Nervous*] I'm not quite sure I follow, Inspector.

DOPPLER: This here on the banisters. It's dried blood.

ANDREW: Blood? Where?

DOPPLER: Here in the angle of the banister—

> [*Warily* ANDREW *crosses to the stairs. He examines the banisters and slowly straightens up. His expression is confused and fearful*]

DOPPLER: Don't touch it, sir! Oh, look sir, here's some more. Someone's been rubbing at the carpet. Do you see, sir? There, deep in the pile, that's blood, sir. Oh! It's still damp. Could you explain how it got there, sir?

ANDREW: I have no idea, Milo . . . er . . . he was a little burnt . . . You must believe me!

DOPPLER: Why should I, sir?

ANDREW: But it's impossible, it was only a game.

DOPPLER: A game, sir? With real bullets and real blood?

ANDREW: [*Gabbling*] There's the hole cut in the pane of glass with the diamond cutter . . . and there are the marks of the ladder on the sill outside . . . and if you look down, you'll see the imprint of the other end of the ladder and of size twenty-eight shoes, or whatever they were, still there in the flower bed and this is the bureau that he broke open . . .

[DOPPLER *descends the stairs*]

DOPPLER: [*Hard*] Thank you, sir, but I don't require a conducted tour. Over the years my eyes have been adequately trained to see things for themselves.

ANDREW: I'm sure they have, Inspector. I only meant to point out facts which would help substantiate my story. And that's the safe we blew open . . .

DOPPLER: Where are the jewels now, sir?

ANDREW: I put them in the bank yesterday.

DOPPLER: On a Saturday?

ANDREW: Yes, Inspector, on a Saturday. I went to Salisbury and I put them in the night safe. I felt they'd be better off there. I mean, anyone could break in and steal them.

DOPPLER: How provident, sir.

ANDREW: And look down the corridor, you'll see the dressing-up basket . . .

[DOPPLER *turns away and looks out of the window, over the garden*]

DOPPLER: You didn't point out that mound of earth in the garden, did you, sir?

[ANDREW *joins* DOPPLER *at the window*]

ANDREW: Mound of earth? What mound of earth?

DOPPLER: Over there—by the far wall. In the shadow of that yew tree. Would you say it had been freshly dug, sir?

ANDREW: [*Shouting*] How the hell should I know. It's probably something the gardener's doing. A new flower bed I think he said.

DOPPLER: A flower bed under a yew tree, sir?

ANDREW: [*Shouting*] I've already told you I don't know. Why don't you ask him yourself? He's probably out there somewhere, maundering around on his moleskinned knees, aching for an opportunity to slander his employer.

DOPPLER: Funny, sir. I've always found gardeners make excellent witnesses. Slow, methodical, positive.

ANDREW: Inspector, I've had just about enough of this farce. Go and dig the damned thing up, if you want to.

DOPPLER: Oh, we shall, sir. Don't worry.

ANDREW: [*Persuasive*] Look, do you really think that I'd bury Tindle in the garden, and leave all that newly turned earth for everyone to find?

DOPPLER: If you weren't expecting us, sir, yes. In a couple of weeks, with some bulbs or a little grass seed, it would be difficult to tell it had ever been disturbed. We in the police know just how fond murderers are of their back gardens, sir.

ANDREW: [*Attempts a laugh*] You're nearer a killer's heart in a garden than anywhere else on earth, eh?

DOPPLER: Except a bedroom, sir. I think you'll find that's still the favorite. [*He starts rummaging in the wardrobe*] Tch! Tch! Tch! What a way to keep clothes! All screwed up at the back of your wardrobe. Why should you do that, I wonder. [*He holds up Milo's shirt*] That's an interesting monogram. I.W. No, I've got it the wrong way up—M.T.

ANDREW: Let me see that.

DOPPLER [*Reading*] Made by Owen and Smith of Percy Street. Sixteen-eight-sixty-nine for Mr. Milo Tindle. Tell me something, sir. [ANDREW *seizes the shirt and stares at it in horror, unable to speak.*

DOPPLER *holds up Milo's jacket and carefully reads the name in the inside pocket*] When Mr. Tindle lurched off as you put it, did he lurch naked?

ANDREW: [*In great distress*] Believe me, Inspector. I have no idea how those clothes got there.

DOPPLER: Didn't you tell me that Mr. Tindle stripped off here the other night to disguise himself as a clown?

ANDREW: Yes, that's right.

DOPPLER: Another part of the humiliation process, I suppose?

ANDREW: But he changed back before he left. I mean, you can't really see him walking through the village dressed as a clown, can you?

DOPPLER: No sir, I can't. Which makes the appearance of his clothes here all the more significant.

ANDREW: It's all so difficult . . .

DOPPLER: On the contrary, sir, I think it's all very simple. I think you started this as a game, exactly as you say you did, in order to play a diabolical trick on Mr. Tindle, but that it went wrong. Your third shot was not a blank as you had supposed,

but was in fact a live bullet which killed Mr. Tindle
stone dead, spattering his blood on the banisters in
the process. When you realized what you'd done,
you panicked and simply buried him in the garden.
It was silly of you not to wash the blood properly
off the banisters and burn his clothes, though.

ANDREW: I swear Tindle left here alive.

DOPPLER: I don't believe it.

ANDREW: I didn't murder him.

DOPPLER: I accept that. As I said, I think it happened
by accident. We'll be quite content with a charge
of manslaughter.

ANDREW: [*Shouting*] I did not kill him! He left here
alive.

DOPPLER: If you will pardon a flippancy, sir, you had
better tell that to the judge.

ANDREW: Look. There's one way of settling this. If you
think Tindle is in the garden, go and dig him up.

DOPPLER: We don't need to find him, sir. Recent deci-
sions have relieved the prosecution of producing the
corpus delicti. If Mr. Tindle is not under the newly
turned earth, it will merely go to indicate that in

your panic you first thought of putting him there, then changed your mind and buried him somewhere else.

ANDREW: Where?

DOPPLER: Does it matter? Spook Spinney! Flasher's Heath! It's all the same to us. He'll turn up sooner or later—discovered by some adulterous salesman or rutting boy scout. And if he doesn't, it scarcely matters, there's so much circumstantial evidence against you. Come along, it's time to go.

ANDREW: [A cry] No!

DOPPLER: I'm afraid I must insist, sir! There's a police car outside.

ANDREW: [Louder] You may have a fleet of police cars out there. I'm not going.

DOPPLER: Now let's have no trouble, sir. Please don't make it difficult.

ANDREW: [Wildly] I must see a lawyer. It's my right.

[ANDREW backs away. DOPPLER makes to seize him, there is a scuffle]

DOPPLER: We can make a call from the station, sir.

We wouldn't want to do anything unconstitutional.
Come on, sir. Don't despair. At the most you'll only
get seven years!

ANDREW: [*Horrified*] Seven years!

DOPPLER: Seven years to regret playing silly games
that go wrong.

ANDREW: [*Bitterly*] It didn't go wrong. It went absolutely right. You've trapped me somehow.

DOPPLER: Yes, sir. You see, we real life detectives
aren't as stupid as we are sometimes portrayed by
writers like yourself. We may not have our pipes, or
orchid houses, our shovel hats or deer-stalkers, but
we tend to be reasonably effective for all that.

ANDREW: Who the hell are you?

DOPPLER: Detective Inspector Doppler, sir, spelled as
in C. Doppler, 1803-1853, whose principle it was
that when the source of any wave movement is approached, the frequency appears greater than it
would to an observer moving away. It is also not
unconnected with Doppler meaning double in Ger-
man—hence Doppleganger or double image. And
of course, for those whose minds run to these things,
it is virtually an anagram of the word Plodder. In-

spector Plodder becomes Inspector Doppler, if you see what I mean, sir!

ANDREW: [*A shriek*] Milo!

MILO: [*Normal voice*] The same.

> [MILO *peels off his disguise which apart from elaborate face and hair make-up—wig, false nose, glasses, cheek padding and moustache —also includes a great deal of body padding, and elevator shoes, which have had the effect of making him taller than* ANDREW, *where in reality he is a fraction shorter*]

ANDREW: You shit!

MILO: Just so.

ANDREW: You platinum-plated, copper-bottomed, dyed-in-the-wool, all-time knock-down drag-out, champion bastard Milo!

MILO: Thanks.

ANDREW: You weasel! You cozening coypu!

MILO: Obliged.

ANDREW: You mendacious bollock of Satan. Milo! You triple-dealing turd!

MILO: In your debt.

ANDREW: Mind you, I'm not saying it wasn't well done. It was—brilliant.

MILO: Thank you.

ANDREW: Have a drink, my dear fellow?

MILO: Let me wash first. I'm covered with make-up and spirit gum.

[ANDREW *shakily pours himself a whisky*]

ANDREW: Just down the corridor. Cheers!

MILO: Good health.

[MILO *exits to bathroom as* ANDREW *gulps drink down*]

ANDREW: Yes, I must say, Milo, I congratulate you. It was first class. You really had me going there for a moment.

MILO: [*Quizzically*] For a moment?

ANDREW: For a long moment, I concede. Of course, I had my suspicions toward the end. Flasher's Heath indeed! That was going a bit far.

MILO: [*Offstage*] I was giving you one of your English sporting chances.

ANDREW: What did you think of *my* performance? The anguish of an innocent man trapped by circumstantial evidence.

MILO: [*Offstage*] Undignified—if it was a performance.

[MILO *returns on stage and picks up his clothes*]

ANDREW: Of course it was, and it had to be undignified to be convincing. As I say, I had my suspicions.

MILO: Indeed? How cleverly you kept them to yourself.

[MILO *goes upstairs to the wardrobe where he dresses in his own clothes*]

ANDREW: And how well you executed it. I loved your Inspector Doppler. His relentless courtesy, his chilly rusticity, his yeoman beadiness.

MILO: [DOPPLER *voice*] I'm glad you view the trifling masquerade in that light, sir.

ANDREW: He was quite a masterpiece. Inspector Ring-rose crossed with a kind of declassé Roger Sheringham, I'd have said.

MILO: Really?

ANDREW: Oh yes! Surely you remember "The Poisoned Chocolate Case," 1929. It was a really astounding tour de force with no less than six separate solutions.

MILO: I've never heard of it.

ANDREW: You should read it. It's a veritable textbook of the literature, not that you need any tips on plotting. I suppose you slipped in here yesterday when I was over in Salisbury.

MILO: Yes, I waited to see you leave.

ANDREW: And dumped the clothes in the wardrobe, and sprinkled a little sacrificial blood on the banisters.

MILO: Exactly. But it wasn't my blood you will be relieved to hear. It was obtained from a pig's liver.

ANDREW: Ugh! Perhaps you will do me the favor of wiping it off in a minute. I don't wish to fertilize the woodworm.

MILO: Question. Where would you find homosexual woodworms?

ANDREW: What?

MILO: In a tallboy. [ANDREW *grimaces. Then, sharply*] I'd like that drink now.

ANDREW: Yes, of course. [*He goes to drinks table and pours a brandy for* MILO] You deserve it.

MILO: [*Sits on chair under staircase*] You know I haven't congratulated you on your game yet. You brought it off with great élan.

ANDREW: Did you think so? Oh good! Good! I must say I was rather delighted with it myself. Tell me . . . did you really think that your last moment on earth had come?

MILO: Yes.

ANDREW: You're not angry, are you?

MILO: Anger is a meaningless word in this context.

ANDREW: I've already tried to explain it to you. I wanted to get to know you—to see if you were, as I suspected, my sort of person.

MILO: A games-playing sort of person?

ANDREW: Exactly.

MILO: And am I?

ANDREW: Most certainly. There's no doubt about it.

MILO: And what exactly is a games-playing person?

ANDREW: He's the complete man—a man of reason and imagination, of potent passions and bright fancies. He's joyous and unrepenting. His weapons are the openness of a child and the cunning of a pike and with them he faces out the black terrors of life. For me personally he is a man who dares to live his life without the crutch of domestic tension. You see, at bottom, I'm rather a solitary man. An arrangement of clouds, the secret mystery of landscape, a game of intrigue and revelation mean more to me than people—even the ones I'm supposed to be in love with. I've never met a woman to whom the claims of intellect were as absolute as they are to me. For a long time I was reticent about all this, knowing that most people would mistake my adroit heart for one of polished stone. But it doesn't worry me any longer. I'm out in the open. I've turned my whole life into one great work of happy invention.

MILO: And you think I'm like this?

ANDREW: Yes, I do.

MILO: You're wrong.

ANDREW: I'm not. Look at the way you chose to get back at me—by playing Inspector Doppler.

MILO: That was just the need for revenge. Every Italian knows about that.

ANDREW: Rubbish. You could have revenged yourself in one of many crude Mafiosi ways—cutting off the gardener's hands, for example, or staking the cleaning woman out on the gravel, or even I suppose, as a last resort, scratched loutish words on the hood of my Bentley. But no, you had to resort to a game.

MILO: I like to pay back in kind.

ANDREW: And is honor satisfied? Is it one set all?

MILO: [*Hard*] By no means. Your game was superior to mine. I merely teased you for a few minutes with the thought of prison. [*Low*] You virtually terrified me to death.

ANDREW: My dear fellow ...

MILO: [*Slowly, thinking it out*] And that changes you profoundly. Once you've given yourself to death, actually faced the fact that the coat sleeve button, the banister, the nail on your fourth finger are the last things you're going to see ever—and then *heard*

91

the sound of your own death—things cannot be the same again. I feel I've been tempered by madness. I stand outside and see myself for the first time without responsibility.

ANDREW: [*Nervous*] That's shock, my dear chap. It'll pass. Here, have another drink. [ANDREW *reaches for the glass.* MILO *jerks away. He is in great distress*] How cold you are. Milo, my dear fellow, I didn't realize how absolutely cold . . .

MILO: So that my only duty is to even our score. That's imperative. As you would put it "I'm three games up in the second set, having lost the first six-love." That's right, isn't it? That's about how you see it? I should hate to cheat.

ANDREW: You're being too modest, Milo. In my scoring it's one set all.

MILO: Oh, no, I can't accept that. You see to the ends of playing the game and drawing honorably level, I *have* killed someone.

ANDREW: Killed someone?

MILO: Murdered someone. Committed murder.

ANDREW: You're not serious.

MILO: Yes.

ANDREW: What is this. Some new murder game?

MILO: Yes. But it has a difference. Both the game and the murder are real. There's absolutely no point in another pretense murder game, is there?

ANDREW: [*Soothing*] No, none. But I don't like to take advantage of you in this emotional state.

MILO: [*Shouting*] It can't wait.

ANDREW: [*Soothing*] All right. All right. Let's play your game. Who did you kill?

MILO: Your girl friend, Teã . . .

ANDREW: You killed Teã?

MILO: [*A little giggle*] She whose cobalt eyes were the secret forest pools of Finlandia. I closed them.

ANDREW: You . . .

MILO: I strangled her—right here on this rug I strangled her and . . . I had her first.

ANDREW: You raped and str . . .

MILO: No. Not rape. She wanted it.

ANDREW: You're lying. You can't take me in with a crude game like this. [*With braggadocio*] Honestly, Milo. You're in the big league now. I gave you credit for better sport than this.

MILO: You'll have all the sport you can stomach in a moment, Andrew. That I promise you.

ANDREW: Really, Milo, I think it would be better if . . .

MILO: When I was here yesterday, planning the blood and clothes for my Inspector Doppler scene, Tea stopped by. I strangled her. She was under that freshly dug mound of earth in the garden that so took Doppler's fancy.

ANDREW: Was? You mean she's not there now?

MILO: No. I moved her.

ANDREW: [*Derisory*] You moved her? Where to? Flasher's Heath, I suppose.

MILO: Something like that. It was too easy leaving her here . . . Too easy for the game you are going to play against the clock before the police arrive.

ANDREW: The police?

MILO: Yes. You see, about an hour ago I phoned them up and asked them to meet me here at ten o'clock tonight. They should be here in about ten minutes.

ANDREW: [*Sarcastic*] Yes, yes. I'm sure they will be. Led, no doubt, by intrepid downy Inspector Doppler.

MILO: Oh, no. It'll be a real policeman, have no fear of that. Detective Sergeant Tarrant, his name is. I told him a lot about you, Andrew. I said that I knew you to be a man obsessed with games-playing and murder considered as a fine art. Your life's great ambition, I said, of which you'd often spoken, was to commit an actual real life murder, hide the body somewhere where it couldn't be traced to you and then leave clues linking you with the crime, strewn about your house in the certain knowledge that the pedestrian and simple-minded police wouldn't recognize them for what they were.

ANDREW: Obsessed with games-playing and murder considered as a fine art! That's rather ingenious of you, Milo. But it won't work. Please sir, Andrew Wyke can't rest until he's committed a real murder which is going to make fools out of all you coppers. Honestly! Tell that to the average desk sergeant and you'll find yourself strapped straight into the giggle jacket.

MILO: Not so in fact, I told them that if they didn't believe me, one look at your bookcase and the furnishings of your house would confirm what I said about your obsessions.

ANDREW: [*Slow*] Go on.

MILO: I also told them that two days ago your girl friend had come to my house in great distress, saying you suspected she was having affairs with other men and had threatened to kill her.

ANDREW: The police believed all that?

MILO: After some demur, yes.

ANDREW: The fuzz are watching too much T.V.

MILO: You mustn't resent imagination in public office, Andrew. Of course, I went on I had no proof that any harm had actually been done to her, but I thought I had better report the matter, particularly as I had just received an excited phone call from you, Andrew, saying you were all set to achieve your life's great ambition.

ANDREW: My dear boy, I quite appreciate you have been captivated by the spirit of games-playing and the need, as you see it, to get even, but frankly you are trying too hard to be a big boy, too soon. [*He goes to the telephone and dials*] Hullo, Joyce, this is Andrew. May I speak to Tẽa . . . she what? . . . when was this? Where . . . ? Oh my God!

> [*He replaces the receiver and takes a drink straight from the bottle.* MILO *is very excited*]

MILO: I told you. I killed her yesterday. Now sweat for your life. You have a little over eight minutes before the law arrives. It's your giant brain against their plodding ones. Concealed in this room are two incriminating clues. And as a final expression of your contempt for the police, you hid the murder weapon itself. Do you follow me so far?

ANDREW: [*Admiringly*] You bastard!

MILO: No judgments please. Three objects. Those you don't find, be sure the police will. I should add that they're all in plain view, though I have somewhat camouflaged them to make the whole thing more fun. The first object is a crystal bracelet.

ANDREW: Not . . .

MILO: Yes, I tore it off her wrist . . . off you go. It's inscribed "From Andrew to Tẽa, a propitiatory offering to a Karelian goddess."

ANDREW: All right! All right! I know how it's inscribed. [*He takes off his jacket and starts his search*]

MILO: Would you like some help?

ANDREW: Yes, damn you!

MILO: Tch! Tch! . . .
"For any man with half an eye.

What stands before him may espy;
But optics sharp it needs I ween,
To see what is not to be seen."

ANDREW: [*Furious*] You said everything was in plain view.

MILO: Well, it's paradoxical old me, isn't it?

ANDREW: I'll get my own back for this . . . don't worry. That I promise you. I'll roast you for this . . . I'll make you so sorry you ever . . .

MILO: Six minutes.

ANDREW: [*Slowly to himself*] I must think . . . I must think . . . It's in plain view, yet not to be seen. H'm . . . there's a visual trick involved.

[ANDREW *searches the room*]

MILO: A propitiatory offering, eh! What was it you had to propitiate for, I ask myself.

ANDREW: None of your bloody business.

MILO: Just for being yourself, I suppose. Just for being cold, torturing Andrew Wyke. Poor Tea, I wonder if all her jewelry was inscribed with apologies for your bully boy behavior.

ANDREW: That's a cheap jibe.

MILO: Mind you, at least you gave her some. Marguerite just had the use of them.

ANDREW: I see what you're doing. You're trying to distract me . . . But you won't succeed . . . I'll solve your puzzle . . . Let me think . . . Optics sharp it needs to see what is not to be seen . . . with the naked eye? It's microscopic! You only see a fraction of it. That's it!

[ANDREW *picks up the microscope and uses it*]

MILO: You won't need the Sherlock Holmes kit, Andrew. The bracelet is full sized and in full view. Though the detective angle is not a bad one. I wonder how your man, Merry*dick*, would have gone about the search.

ANDREW: [*Furious*] Merrydew! St. Lord John Merrydew!

MILO: Perhaps he'd have clambered up on that desk to look at the plinth, hauling his great tun of port belly after him. [ANDREW *climbs up on his desk to inspect the plinth*] Or perhaps he'd have gone straight to the chimney and shoved his fat Father Christmas face right up to it. [ANDREW *runs to the chimney and climbs inside it*] "My God!" cried the noble Lord, puking on his pipe and indulging his famed taste for bad puns. "This is hardly a *sootable* place for a gentleman!"

ANDREW: [*Emerges from the chimney*] I won't listen to you. I must think . . . What are the properties of crystal? It's hard . . . It's brilliant . . . It's transparent.

MILO: You're getting warm, Andrew.

ANDREW: You look through it and you don't see it. Now the only place to conceal a transparent thing, so as to make it invisible yet keep it in plain view, is in another transparent thing like . . . [*He inspects various glass objects including* MILO's *drink which he is holding conspicuously. Finally he crosses to the ornamental tank and lifts out the bracelet*] Suddenly it's all as clear as crystal. I don't need to destroy this, do I? She could have this here anytime.

MILO: True, it was only planted so that the police could read the inscription. At least they'd know that your relationship with Teã hadn't always been a happy one.

ANDREW: Very subtle. What next?

MILO: The next object is much more damning. The clue is a riddle, which goes as follows:

> "Two brothers we are,
> Great burdens we bear,
> On which we are bitterly pressed.
> The truth is to say,
> We are full all the day,
> And empty when we go to rest."

ANDREW: Oh, I know that . . . don't tell me . . . full all the day, empty when we go to rest . . . it's a . . . it's a pair of shoes!

MILO: Very good. In this case, one right, high-heeled shoe. Size six. The other, I need hardly add, is on Teã's body.

ANDREW: Oh, my God. Poor Teã. [*He searches the room*]

MILO: Poor Teã, eh? Well, that's a bit better. It's the first sign of sorrow you've shown since you heard of her death.

ANDREW: It's not true! You think I don't care about Teã, don't you? But I must save myself.

MILO: You're loving it. You're in a high state of brilliance and excitement. The thought that you are playing a game for your life is practically giving you an orgasm. It's pitiable.

ANDREW: Hold your filthy tongue. What you see before you is someone using a mighty control to keep terror in check, while he tries to solve a particularly sadistic and morbid puzzle. It's a triumph of the mind over atavism! [ANDREW *searches under the stairs and in the bookshelves, and pipe racks then the sailor's foot and finally finds the shoe in a brightly decorated cornucopia attached to the stage left column*] Ah! What have we here?

MILO: Very good! Sorry it's so messy. It's only earth from Tea's first grave in your garden.

[ANDREW *burns the shoe in the stove*]

ANDREW: Now there's one thing left, isn't there. The murder weapon, that's what you said. Now you strangled her here. What with? Let's see . . . a rope . . . a belt . . . a scarf . . .

MILO: It bit into her neck very deeply, Andrew. I had to pry it loose.

ANDREW: You sadistic bloody wop!

MILO: I hope I didn't hear that correctly . . . It would

be foolish to antagonize me at this stage. Because as you're certain to need a lot more help, I would hate to have to give you an oblique, Florentine sort of one, sewn with treachery and double dealing.

ANDREW: [*Controlling himself*] All right! All right!

MILO: As Don Quixote in common with a great number of chaps remarked, "*No es Oro todo que reluce.*"

ANDREW: But the other chaps, of course, didn't say it in Spanish, did they?

MILO: Well at least you know it was Spanish, even if you can't speak it. I suppose that's what is meant by a general education in England.

ANDREW: God, you're pretty damned insufferable, Milo.

MILO: I've learned it. Let's try you on a little Latin. Every gentleman knows Latin. I'm sure you're acquainted with the Winchester College Hall Book of 1401?

ANDREW: [*Sarcastic*] Naturally. As a matter of fact I've got the paperback by my bedside.

MILO: [*Bland*] Then you will remember an entry by Alanus De Insulis—"*Non teneas nurum totum quod splendet ut aurum.*"

ANDREW: [*Sarcastic*] I'm afraid I can't have got that far yet.

MILO: Pity . . . I suppose I could put it another way. "*Que tout n'est pas or qu'on voit luire.*" The French, of course, is thirteenth century.

ANDREW: Say it again, slowly.

MILO: All-that-glitters . . .

ANDREW: All that glitters isn't gold . . . Why didn't you say that in the first place . . . [MILO *whistles a scale*] Golden notes? Golden whistle? . . . Golden cord? . . . Golden cord! You strangled her with a golden cord and put it round the bellpull. [ANDREW *runs to the bellpull examines it, but finds nothing*] No, you didn't. [MILO *whistles "Anything Goes"*] Anything goes. In olden d . . . In olden days a . . . glimpse of stocking. It's in the spin dryer. [ANDREW *goes off down the corridor to kitchen*]

MILO: Cold, cold. It's in this room, remember.

ANDREW: [*Returning*] Where do you put stockings? On legs, golden legs . . . [*He examines the golden legs of the fender, then a chair*]

MILO: [*Sings*] "In olden days a glimpse of stocking was looked on as something shocking . . ." I thought

I heard something. [*He exits to hallway. A moment later, he returns*] Yes, Andrew, it's the police. They're coming up the drive.

ANDREW: [*Desperate*] Keep them out! Give me one more minute!

MILO: A glimpse of stocking, remember.

[MILO *exits to hallway*]

MILO: [*Offstage*] Good evening, Detective Sergeant Tarrant.

TARRANT: [*Offstage*] Yes, sir. This is Constable Higgs.

MILO: [*Off*] Good evening, Constable.

HIGGS: Good evening, sir.

[*The grandfather clock strikes ten*]

ANDREW: Olden days ... A glimpse ... Now you see it now you don't! Of course, the clock. [*He rushes to clock and finds stocking*]

MILO: [*Off*] Nice of you to be so prompt. I apologize for keeping you waiting out there for a moment. The front door's a bit stiff.

TARRANT: [*Off*] That's all right, sir. We're used to waiting.

MILO: Won't you hang your coats up? It's a bit warm inside.

TARRANT: Thank you, sir. I expect we'll be here a little time.

[ANDREW *puts stocking into fire*]

MILO: [*Off*] Here, Constable. Let me take your helmet.

HIGGS: Thank you, sir. If it's all the same to you, I think I'll keep it with me, but I'll take my coat off.

[*Door slams offstage*]

MILO: [*Off*] Come in, gentlemen. May I introduce Mr. Andrew Wyke. Andrew, may I introduce Detective Sergeant Tarrant and Constable Higgs.

ANDREW: [*Calls*] Come in, gentlemen, come in.

[*A pause. No one enters*]

MILO: [*Off*] Or perhaps I should say, Inspector Plodder and Constable Freshface. Thank you, Sergeant. We won't be needing you after all.

TARRANT: That's all right, sir. Better to be safe than sorry, that's what I say, Good night, sir.

MILO: [*Own voice*] Good night, Sergeant. Good night Constable. Good night, sir.

[MILO *returns from hallway.* ANDREW *sinks on the settee, shattered*]

MILO: Aren't you going to ask about Tea? She did call here yesterday looking for you when I was here setting the Doppler scene. I told her about the trick you had played on me with the gun. She wasn't a bit surprised. She knows only too well the kind of games you play—the kind of humiliation you enjoy inflicting on people. I said I wanted to play a game to get even with you, and I asked her to help me. I asked her to lend me a stocking, a shoe and a bracelet. She collaborated with enthusiasm. So did her flat-mate, Joyce. Would you like to telephone her, she'll talk to you now? Of course you don't really have much to say to her, do you? She's not really your mistress. She told me you and she hadn't slept together for over a year. She told me you were practically impotent—not at all, in fact, the selector's choice for the next Olympics.

[ANDREW *hides his head as* MILO *starts up the stairs*]

ANDREW: Where are you going?

MILO: To collect Marguerite's fur coat.

ANDREW: She's not coming back?

MILO: No. Among other things she said she was fed up with living in Hamleys.

ANDREW: Hamleys?

MILO: It's a toy shop in Regent Street.

ANDREW: Milo.

MILO: Yes?

ANDREW: Don't go. Don't waste it all on Marguerite. She doesn't appreciate you like I do. You and I are evenly matched. We know what it is to play a game and that's so rare. Two people coming together who have the courage to spend the little time of light between the eternal darkness—joking.

MILO: Do you mean live here?

ANDREW: Yes.

MILO: [*Scornfully*] Is it legal in private between two consenting games-players?

ANDREW: Please . . . I just want someone to play with.

MILO: No.

ANDREW: Please.

MILO: No. Most people want someone to *live* with. But you have no life to give anyone—only the tricks and the shadows of long ago. Take a look at yourself, Andrew, and ask yourself a few simple questions about your attachment to the English detective story. Perhaps you might come to realize that the only place you can inhabit is a dead world—a country house world where peers and colonels die in their studies; where butlers steal the port, and pert parlormaids cringe, weeping malapropisms behind green baize doors. It's a world of coldness and class hatred, and two-dimensional characters who are not expected to communicate; it's a world where only the amateurs win, and where foreigners are automatically figures of fun. To be *puzzled* is all. Forgive me for taking Marguerite to a life where people try to *understand*. To put it shortly, the detective story is the normal recreation of snobbish, outdated, life-hating, ignoble minds. I'll get that fur coat now. I presume it is Marguerite's, unless, that is, you've taken to tranvestism as a substitute for non-performance.

[MILO *disappears into the bedroom.* ANDREW *sits on below, crushed and humiliated. After a minute, he rises and starts wearily across the stage. Suddenly he stops as a thought enters his mind*]

ANDREW: [*To himself*] The coat! . . . The fur coat . . . of course . . . I've got him! [*He brightens visibly— a man who realizes suddenly that he can rescue a victory out of the jaws of defeat—and crosses firmly to his desk and takes out his gun*] You see, Inspector, I was working in the morning room when I heard a noise. I seized my gun and came in here. I saw the figure of a man, apparently carrying my wife's fur coat. I shouted for him to put his hands up, but instead he ran toward the front door, trying to escape. Though I aimed low, I'm afraid I shot him dead. [*Inspector's voice*] Mustn't blame yourself, sir, could have happened to anybody!

[MILO *returns, carrying fur coat. He comes down the stairs, but does not see the gun hidden behind* ANDREW'S *back*]

ANDREW: I'm not going to let you go, you know.

MILO: No? What are you going to do, Andrew. Shoot me down? Play that old burglar game again?

110

ANDREW: Yes, that's precisely what I could do.

MILO: It wouldn't work, you know, even if you had the guts to go through with it.

ANDREW: Why not?

MILO: [*Fetches a suitcase from the hall and packs the fur coat*] Because of what happened when I left here on Friday night. I *lurched* home in the moonlight, numb and dazed, and soiled. I sat up all night in a chair—damaged—contaminated by you and this house. I remembered something my father said to me; "In this country, Milo," he said, "there's justice, but sometimes for a foreigner it is difficult." In the morning I went to the police station and told them what had happened. One of them—Sergeant Tarrant—yes, he's real—took me into a room and we had quite a long chat. But I don't think he really believed me, even though I showed him the powder burn on my head. He seemed more interested in my relationship with Marguerite, which by the way they all appeared to know about. I felt this terrible anger coming over me. I thought "they're not going to believe me because I'm a stranger from London who's screwing the wife of the local nob and has got what he deserved." So I thought of my father,

111

and what I might have done in Italy, and I took my own revenge. But remember, Andrew, the police might still come.

ANDREW: [*Slowly*] Then why haven't they, then?

MILO: I don't know, perhaps they won't. But even if they don't, you can't play your burglar game now; they'd never swallow it. So you see, you've lost.

ANDREW: I don't believe one word you're saying.

MILO: [*Deliberately*] It's the truth.

ANDREW: You're lying!

MILO: Why don't you phone Sergeant Tarrant if you don't believe me.

ANDREW: And say what? Please, Sergeant, has Milo Tindle been in saying that I framed him as a burglar and then shot him? I'm not that half-witted.

MILO: Suit yourself.

ANDREW: I shall shoot you, Milo. You come here and ask my permission to steal away my wife, you pry into my manhood, you lecture me on dead worlds and ignoble minds, and you mock Merridew. Well, they're all real bullets this time.

MILO: I'm going home now.

[MILO *starts to leave,* ANDREW *fires.* MILO *drops in pain, fatally shot.* ANDREW *kneels and holds his head up*]

ANDREW: You're a bad liar, Milo, and in the final analysis, an uninventive games-player. Can you hear me? Then listen to this, NEVER play the same game three times running.

[*There is the sound of a car approaching and pulling to a halt. A flashing blue police car light shines through the window. The door bell rings. There is a loud knocking on door. Painfully* MILO *lifts his head from the floor, he laughs*]

MILO: Game, set and match!

[*His laugh becomes a cough. Blood trickles from his mouth. He grimaces in surprise at the pain and dies. The knocking on the door is repeated more loudly.* ANDREW *staggers to his desk and accidentally presses the button on it. This sets off the sailor who laughs ironically. The knocking becomes more insistent.* ANDREW *leans weakly against pillar. He shouts in anguish as*]

THE CURTAIN FALLS

ABOUT THE AUTHOR

ANTHONY SHAFFER graduated from Cambridge, where he was editor of the university magazine *Granta*, in 1950. After three years as a barrister, he decided to enter journalism and started writing commercials, documentaries, and television dramas. He has written three screen plays, the first of which, *Fourbrush and the Penguins*, is presently being filmed in the Antarctic. Mr. Schaffer has also written the film script for his twin brother Peter Shaffer's original stage play *Black Comedy*, and has collaborated with Peter with several detective novels. SLEUTH is Anthony Shaffer's first play for the legitimate theatre.

Mr. Shaffer is married to ex-model Carolyn Soley and has two young daughters. He divides his time between London and Somerset.